RIPPLES IN THE STREAM

A Pragmatic Journey Through
Gautama Buddha's Teachings

KARMA YESHE RABGYE

Ripples In The Stream

© November 2015

by Karma Yeshe Rabgye

ISBN - 13: 978-1518689864

ISBN - 10: 1518689868

For more information on author Karama Yeshe Rabgye, visit

www.buddhismguide.org.

Cover artwork by: Prodesignsx

Interior design by: Melissa@thewriterlab.com

First Edition for Print November 2015

www.buddhismguide.org

This book is dedicated to 'my boys'
(Nyima, Dawwa, Tenzin, Paljor, Jigten, Rabjor & Deepak)
Thank you for all the joy you have given me and for making my
life worth living.

Also From The Author

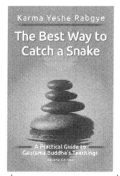

Buddhism, with its stress on non-violence, the 'middle path' and its promise of nirvana, finds many followers. But in today's world, it has become simply a fad for some, something to follow because their favourite celebrity is doing so. Wearing robes or carrying prayer beads does not make one a Buddhist; it has to be ingrained within, and should become a part of one's daily life. The Best Way to Catch a Snake, a three-part volume, is a beginner's guide to Buddhism for all those who want to start their journey towards nirvana but don't know how and where. It goes beyond the exotic rituals and practices that Buddhism today has become all about, and looks at the fundamental tenets that, without a knowledge of, one cannot be a Buddhist. It elucidates the Four Seals, the Four Noble Truths, and the Four Thoughts of Buddhism in simple, jargon-free language. The author, a Buddhist monk himself, combines examples from his own experience with simple exercises to skilfully guide you through the Buddha's teachings. An easily relatable and valuable source of Buddhist knowledge, this book is a must for anyone drawn to Gautama Buddha's teachings.

Achieve a life of balance with Karma Yeshe Rabgye's eye-opening second book, Life's Meandering Path. The thirty-eight principles set forth, based on the teachings of Gautama Buddha, comprise a basic guide to living for anyone seeking peace and harmony. The value of such qualities as individual responsibility, rational thought and the fulfilment of social obligations are discussed—as well as exactly how to implement each of these principles into one's daily life. It is not uncommon to experience a sense of fear or uncertainty in the oftentimes frantic, fast-paced world in which we live. But it is possible to move beyond these obstacles and that feeling of being overwhelmed, into a state where happiness and a lack of suffering dominate. Learn how to juggle individual challenges, family obligations, social responsibility and personal growth while maintaining a vital sense of balance in the midst of a chaotic world. All of this is possible without needing to call oneself a Buddhist or Christian or Muslim. Regardless of religion or faith, readers will learn how to achieve some much needed peace in this enriching guide to life.

Contents

Introduction

In 2012 I published my first book, and shortly after, I started writing a blog. I wanted to try and move Gautama Buddha's teachings away from dogma, mysticism and the ritual practices that have been added to them over the years. I truly believe his teachings are more to do with how to live our life, and not a religion that should be blindly followed.

I wanted to explore his teachings in a pragmatic and contemporary way. They have completely changed my life and I wished to share my thoughts, experiences and conclusions with others who are, like me, searching for a better way to live their life.

I did not, and would not, belittle the traditional teachings of Gautama Buddha, as these were the foundation of my many years of Buddhist study. However, I wanted my blog to be relevant to everyone, no matter what their religion, education or culture.

In this book, I have compiled many, but not all, of my blog posts over a three year period. Some have been updated and slightly revised. I hope you find them informative, thought provoking and applicable to your life. This is not a scholarly book and all I am trying to do is drop a pebble into the pool of Buddhism and cause a few ripples within your mind stream. How far you follow those ripples is up to you.

The book covers such diverse subjects as Gautama Buddha's early teachings, mindfulness, meditation, euthanasia, superstitions, homosexuality, forgiveness, positivity and much more besides.

You can find all my blog posts, guided meditation practices, teaching videos and podcasts on my website: **www.buddhismguide.org**.

If you would like to contact me about something you have read in this book, or just to give me feedback, please email me at **buddhismguide@yahoo.com**.

Karma Yeshe Rabgye

1

Gautama Buddha's First Teaching

Gautama Buddha's first teaching was on the four noble truths, and it still remains the very foundation on which Buddhism is built.

The first noble truth is 'There is suffering.' There is big discussion about the translation of the word suffering, but as nobody has ever come up with a better word, we'll stick with it. However, just to make things clear, suffering here means a dissatisfaction, discontentment, an uneasy feeling running through our lives.

Gautama Buddha stated that there are three types of suffering:

Firstly, the suffering of pain. This one is easy for us to understand, as it is our daily suffering. It is when we have a headache, cold, hangover and so on. This is the physical side of the suffering, but there is also a mental side as well. We may be feeling lonely because someone has left us, or we may be feeling sad because someone has died. These are all the suffering of pain.

Secondly, we have the suffering of happiness. Now this one is a bit harder for us to understand. When we are happy we never think about suffering, but it is there just lurking around the corner. Let's look at some examples:

You buy a new iPad and you are so happy. You show it to your family and friends who are envious. You take this iPad everywhere with you and use it every day to play games, surf the net, watch films and so on. You could not be happier. Then one day you can't find it. It has been stolen. Now that happiness you had has changed into sadness – this is the suffering of happiness.

Another example is, you are on the metro sitting opposite the most beautiful person you have ever seen. You start talking and arrange to meet up later that week for a drink. After a while you become lovers and eventually marry. Your life is total bliss. You are married to the most beautiful person in the world. You couldn't be happier. Then one day he/she meets someone else and leaves you. Now your happiness has changed and you are feeling sad and angry – this is the suffering of happiness.

The third suffering is the all-pervasive suffering. This type of suffering is within everything in our lives, but because it is suffering on a subtle level, we are prone to missing it. This type of suffering is a condition that exists because of how we perceive ourselves in relation to the world. So you could say that our entire worldly experience is a definition of suffering that we cannot even see.

So how do we see ourselves and the world? Well, we see them as separate – I'm here and the world is outside of me. In other words, as subject and object. We see ourselves as a solid, independent self.

But Buddha taught that this is not true and we are actually the coming together of five things, namely, the five aggregates. This may sound a little odd but I will explain this point in my next posting.

So the way we look at things, subject and object, me and everything else, is in some way the cause of our suffering that will come to us in the future. It is like eating a wonderful meal but not knowing it has been poisoned. Whilst we are eating the food we are happy, but later on, once the poison starts to work, we suffer.

So why did Gautama Buddha want us to know that our lives have suffering in them? Was he trying to depress us? Was he a killjoy? No, the reason he taught this was to help us understand that we have a problem. If we don't know we have a problem, we will not look for a solution. It is the same as if we don't know we are sick, we will not go to the doctor. If we know we are sick we go to the doctor and he will tell us what is making us sick, and gives us medicine to cure it. It is the same here. If we know we are suffering we will look for the cause and the cure.

So, Gautama Buddha was showing us that we have a problem. We have to fully understand this point. If we do fully understand it we will be able to move on to the next noble truths, which explain the causes of our suffering and how we can reduce it.

2

How We Experience the World

In the previous post I mentioned the five aggregates, so here is a brief description of each aggregate.

The aggregates are form, feeling, conception, mental formation and consciousness.

Form, or matter, corresponds to physical factors, which not only includes our own bodies, but also the material objects that surround us. Form also includes the five physical sense organs and their corresponding physical objects. The five physical sense organs are eye, ear, nose, tongue and body. Their corresponding objects are visible form, sound, smell, taste and touch.

Feeling is the second aggregate and it can be divided into three different types of experience, namely pleasant, unpleasant or neutral. One of these three feelings are present in every experience we have, whether we are aware of them or not.

There are six kinds of experience, five physical and one mental. The experiences happen when your eye contacts with a visible form, your ear with sound, your nose with smell, your tongue with taste and your body with any other tangible object.

These are the five physical experiences. The mental experience is when your mind is in contact with mental objects, such as ideas and thoughts.

Our feelings are extremely important as, in the end, they determine what we experience. We all want good feelings and try to avoid bad feelings.

The third aggregate is conception and this is where we attach a name to an experience. Here, we formulate a conception of an idea about the object we perceive. The purpose of this aggregate is to analyse and investigate. When we come into contact with an object, our conception aggregate categorises it by shape, colour, motion, location, sex and other such categories. These arise as concepts which we are either born with or have added. Concepts can come from parents, school, society, friends and other social groups. Everything we have learnt or are learning, including in this book, form our concepts.

The fourth aggregate is mental formation. It is the impression created by previous actions. This aggregate starts in the mind and is then reflected in our body and speech. That means whatever action we do in this life is part of this aggregate.

Maybe a better way to call this aggregate is mental formation and volition. Volition is the capability of conscious choice, decision and intention. So the mental formation stems from our past, and volition, from the present moment. Both function together to determine our response to an object of experience. These responses have moral consequences in the sense of skilful, unskilful and neutral acts.

The final aggregate is consciousness, which is extremely powerful, and from this stem the third and fourth aggregates. It is mere awareness of an object. When the eyes and a visible object come into contact, the eye consciousness will become associated with that object and visual consciousness will arise. It is the same with all the six consciousnesses.

It should be noted that consciousness is not personal experience, but merely awareness of an object. Personal experiences are produced through the functioning of the feeling aggregate, the conception aggregate and the mental formation aggregate. These three turn mere awareness into a personal experience.

This all sounds a bit dry and confusing, so lets put this all together. Your eyes see the form. Your consciousness becomes aware of it. Your conception identifies it. A pleasant, unpleasant or neutral feeling arises. Your mental formation makes you respond to it with a conditioned reaction, stemming from your past.

In the Khandha Sutra Gautama Buddha called them the five clinging aggregates and this is where the problem comes for us. We cling to these aggregates as though they are the self – a solid and permanent you. However, Gautama Buddha taught non-self. When these five aggregates come together we experience the world, but when they disperse we stop experiencing the world. He also taught us that there is absolutely no experience other than these five aggregates. These aggregates are ever-changing and so there really isn't anything solid for us to cling to. When we try to cling to them as a permanent self we suffer, and this is what Gautama Buddha was pointing out in the first noble truth.

3

Gautama Buddha's Second Truth

In the first truth Gautama Buddha encouraged us to fully understand that there is suffering in every corner of our lives. In his second truth he tells us what causes these sufferings.

There is no one cause of our suffering. Just as there is no one cause of anything. The cause of suffering people talk about the most is craving. However, in this posting I want to focus on the three poisons. These are desire, aversion/anger and unawareness. Let's look at these mental defilements individually.

Desire – Our desires are never-ending. Once we have something new, we start wanting something else. Gautama Buddha put it this way in the Vaipulya Sutra:

> 'Human desires are endless. It is like the thirst of a man who drinks salt water: he gets no satisfaction and his thirst is only increased.'

This is because we wrongly believe that material things can make us permanently and truly happy. If we investigate, we will find that our desires eventually lead us into a feeling of discontentment. There is no problem in desiring things and trying to make our lives more comfortable; the problem is clinging and grasping at these desires. We get attached to things and when they break, are stolen or die – which they inevitably will – we become discontented, unhappy and ill at ease.

To break this cycle we have to see things as they really are, impermanent. Things come into being when the causes and conditions are correct. Once these causes and conditions change, as they will because they are impermanent, the thing also changes or dies. So if we understand this we will not become attached to things, which in turn will end that particular type of suffering.

Anger and Aversion – Aversion is the opposite of attachment, and anger leads to hatred, discrimination, aggression and a lack of compassion. Neither are helpful emotions. With desire we want to cling to objects, but with aversion we do the exact opposite. We spend all our time and energy trying to push the thing away that we do not like. As with desire, we just need to let go, not hold on to this aversion. Don't engage with it, hold it or repress it – simply acknowledge you have an aversion for it and then let it go.

If we do not acknowledge our aversions we are just falling into denial, and this again is not good for our state of mind. So, just watch the aversion rise and fall – do not engage with it. Just work at letting it go.

Some say that anger is natural and should be expressed at all costs. This is because most people only see two ways of dealing with anger, that is, express or repress. Both are unhealthy. If you express it, it can lead to violence, hatred and people's feelings being hurt, or even worse, if you are the leader of a country, it can lead to war and genocide. If you repress it, you are just storing up trouble for the future. You may be able to keep it down for some time, but eventually it will surface and may even come back more violent and hurtful.

Anger is such a destructive emotion because we engage with it and let it take control of us. So, Gautama Buddha had a different idea. He advised us to look at the anger and see where it comes from. It is not to be dealt with, but observed. If we do this, we will see that it stems from our exaggerating the negative qualities of someone or projecting negative qualities that are not actually there, on to someone or something.

One of the best ways of counteracting anger is patience. This is the opposite of anger. We should not react straight away, but should count to ten and spend some time reflecting on the situation. This will help us calm down and see things more rationally. Of course, this is not a simple thing to do when one is wrapped up in the moment. So the best thing to do is at the end of the day, look back on when you became angry. See how you could have acted more calmly and imagine what the outcome may have been if you had. Slowly, you will learn not to react instantly but to first reflect.

Unawareness – Here, unawareness means lack of understanding of the true nature of things, which leads us to having wrong views. In theAvatamsaka Sutra, Gautama Buddha said:

> 'Because of their unawareness, people are always thinking wrong thoughts and always losing the right viewpoint and, clinging to their egos, they take wrong actions. As a result, they become attached to a delusive existence.'

This is an extremely important point, because if you have a wrong view, it will lead you onto a wrong path and you will get a wrong outcome. In Buddhism, we are looking for freedom or liberation from suffering, discontentment and the unease that runs throughout our lives, but if we do not understand what is causing our suffering how do we eliminate it?

So unawareness means a lack of knowledge, and we have all been in that position. It can take on many forms – if you do not understand another person's culture and discriminate against them, if you are not educated and someone fools you into giving up your life savings, if you did not understand what someone was saying and you get angry with them, if you sacrifice animals to a god so as to obtain wealth or good crops or if you blindly follow a religious practice.

The way out of unawareness is to gain knowledge, to ask questions so as to clear up any doubts and then meditate on this knowledge. This will turn your knowledge into wisdom. Knowledge is learnt,

but wisdom transcends knowledge and becomes the way you are, the way you act, your very essence. It is true understanding, not something stemming from your intellect.

These three poisons need to be understood and then abandoned. In the Cula-dukkhakkhandha Sutra, Gautama Buddha stated that it is not enough to just understand the three poisons. He stated that until we abandon them they will keep returning.

4

Everything Must Change

In the last posting I mentioned unawareness. So, what are the things we are unaware of? Usually, in Buddhism, they talk about three main things, namely suffering, non-self and impermanence. I have covered suffering in the post entitled 'Gautama Buddha's First Truth,' and non-self was covered in the post called 'How We Experience the World.' So I will talk about the third one, impermanence, in this posting.

> Whatever is born is impermanent and is bound to die. Whatever is stored up is impermanent and is bound to run out. Whatever comes together is impermanent and is bound to come apart. Whatever is built is impermanent and is bound to collapse. Whatever rises up is impermanent and is bound to fall down. So also, friendship and enmity, fortune and sorrow, good and evil, all the thoughts that run through your mind – everything is always changing.
> (Patrul Rinpoche – Words of My Perfect Teacher)

In Tibetan Buddhism there are Four Seals, and the first seal is 'All compounded things are impermanent.' Now, at first glance that seems a tad depressing. However, if we look closely and contemplate the meaning it turns out to be a breath of fresh air.

The definition of compounded is 'something that consists of two or more things combined together.' All phenomena is compounded, and that includes you and me. Just think for a moment, is there anything in this universe that isn't compounded? As of yet we haven't found anything.

The point Gautama Buddha was making here is that anything that is made up of a combination of other things will eventually fall apart. It will come into being when the various causes and conditions are right, it will exist for a certain amount of time, and then it will disintegrate – this is the nature of all things, this is impermanence. It is an undeniable and inescapable fact of life.

Impermanence isn't a word we readily warm to, and it would be much nicer for us to believe that everything is permanent. But this simply isn't true, and in order to stop our suffering, we need to acknowledge this fact. The reason we do not like to hear about impermanence is because it brings up visions of sickness, pain, disintegration and death. We get a horrible sick feeling in our stomachs because we equate impermanence with loss – loss of a loved one, loss of our friends or even loss of something as trivial as our iphone. So, it is vitally important for all of us to understand impermanence.

Why is it important? What are the benefits of understanding it? It means we will achieve freedom from fear, freedom from suffering and freedom from panic, because when we know things are not going to last, we are free of any fear, agony or pain of losing something or someone.

Our mistaken belief is that things come into existence on their own, and last forever. This kind of mistaken belief causes us to cling to worldly possessions, such as material objects, the search for pleasure, recognition, honour and so on. It causes pride, attachment, aversion and arrogance to grow within us because we truly believe things are here to stay. We grow completely attached to the concerns of this life.

So it's a relief when we finally understand that everything is impermanent and we can't do a thing to change that fact. We can now let go and relax our grip on things – that's a real breath of fresh air!

Impermanence is not only true for pleasurable things, but for painful things as well. Maybe someone you care for has died or left you, and you are sad and lonely. These emotions are also impermanent and so will, after time, also change. All the things we have aversion towards will only last a short time. Like the morning dew, it will all soon change and disappear.

Like the dew that remains for a moment or two on the tips of the grass and then melts with the dawn. The pleasures we find in the course of our lives last only an instant, they cannot endure.

(Thogme Zangpo – Thirty-Seven Practices of All Buddha's Sons)

5

Gautama Buddha's Third Truth

This truth is called nirvana, liberation, enlightenment and so on. It is hotly debated these days. Some think that if you reach nirvana you will never be born again, others think you will be reborn but you can pick where. For people who do not believe in rebirth, they see it as something we can achieve in this lifetime. I have no idea who is right and who is wrong – it may be they are all wrong. I will just write my own thoughts here and you can decide for yourselves what you believe. I will show you that there are two good bits of news in this third noble truth.

I do not see nirvana as some mystical or metaphysical thing. I do believe it is beyond our concepts of right and wrong, good and bad, existence and non-existence. All these are positions relative to each other, mere labels created by language. This means it cannot be fully realised through language alone, and is only reached through meditation and implementation.

Gautama Buddha said that nirvana is the 'highest happiness', but he wasn't talking about the mundane happiness we strive for in our everyday lives. He was talking about absolute freedom from evil, freedom from craving, attachment, desire, hatred and unawareness. All of this we can achieve in this lifetime by truly understanding the four noble truths and following the eightfold path. Once we start meditating on these teachings and turning them from knowledge into wisdom, we will start to change our actions of body, speech and mind. Knowledge is something learned, something intellectual, where as wisdom is a part of our lives.

So this is the first bit of good news. Nirvana can be reached by anyone, in this very lifetime, whether they call themselves Buddhist or not – you just have to put in the effort.

People think that nirvana is like heaven, full of happiness, the opposite of this world. They imagine that there, the sun shines brightly every day, and only 'good' people are around, one doesn't have to work, there are no money worries, everybody is friendly and every moment is filled with happiness. However, this is just a projection of our dualistic minds, trying to fill heaven with all the things we like best. But what about all the things other people like and we don't? I would want a heaven where no one eats meat, while others would want one where they could eat a big fat juicy steak every day. Do we each get a heaven of our own? I believe if people really gave some thought to their concept of heaven, they would understand they were just changing one conditioned world for another, and in that way, heaven, like this world, would be equally impermanent.

So this is the second bit of good news; we do not have to die to attain nirvana. It can be obtained during this lifetime. Death is irrelevant to nirvana. People feel like this life is full of discontentment and causes them nothing but suffering, and the only way out is death. They feel at death they will be miraculously transported to a better place. But nirvana isn't a place; it is the cessation of the three poisons, namely, desire, aversion and unawareness. Gautama Buddha defined it as 'perfect peace', or a state of mind that is free from craving, anger and other afflictive states.

So in a nut shell, I believe nirvana isn't a metaphysical thing, it isn't a place to go to and we do not have to die to realise nirvana. It is an extinguishing of our afflictive states of mind and can be reached by anyone in this very lifetime.

6

Looking Back, So You Can Move Forward

Many years ago when I first moved to India, I went to see a Buddhist teacher to get a personal instruction. We chatted for around thirty minutes, and then he told me at the end of each day to sit quietly and review all my actions, thoughts, feelings and emotions for that day. Think of what was good and what was not good: the things that were less good I should make a conscious effort to avoid doing again, and the good things I should make a conscious effort to continue doing. I wasn't very impressed at first as I was looking for something a bit more magical, but after carrying out the instructions for a few days, I started to get the point. What he was asking me to do was take responsibility for my actions and understand what is driving me to make those actions. I think it was the one single thing that has helped me the most in my life, and I am forever indebted to this teacher.

Gautama Buddha gave his son, Rahula, similar advice. He asked him what a mirror is for, and his son answered for reflecting. Gautama Buddha then states:

'In the same way, Rahula, bodily action should be done with reflection and consideration; verbal action should be done with reflection and consideration; mental action should be done with reflection and consideration.

'Purify bodily action through repeated consideration and review; purify verbal action through repeated consideration and review; purify mental action through repeated consideration and review'.

Gautama Buddha was talking about reviewing our actions of body, speech and mind, and this is what I am also suggesting here. Do daily reviews before you go to bed. Find a quiet place to sit and work through your day. You do not have to be sitting on the floor, but from my experience, I think it is better to be sitting in an upright position, so you do not fall asleep.

So that you are present in the moment, do the three breath-calming techniques. This entails taking three deep breaths. When you breathe in, take a really deep breath that goes right down inside, and when you breathe out, be sure you expel all of the air inside you. If you do this three times you will feel relaxed, focused and present in the moment

Now start to look at your actions of body, speech and mind from that day. Look at the good and not-so-good situations. Be honest with yourself, or there will be very little benefit. Try and get into a habit of reviewing your thoughts, feelings and emotions on a daily basis.

We go through life at such breakneck speed and never take time to stop and examine our thoughts, feelings and emotions. We just seem to accept them. We say things like, 'I have always been an angry person', 'I've been jealous since I was a kid', or 'I hate this and love that' —we never look at why that is or try to change it. This daily review will help you stop and look at what is driving these emotions and feelings. It will help you to respond instead of react to situations.

If we do stop and look, we may be surprised at what is driving us. It could be a throwback from your childhood and, because you are now an adult, it has become an outdated way to be. So use this review session as a mechanism for change, but remember change can only come through understanding. The review session is a way for us to understand our inner workings.

When you look back and find a situation in which you didn't act in a helpful way, look at what thoughts, feelings and emotions surrounded that act. What drove you to act in such a way? Was it jealousy, pride, fear, anger, pleasure or pain? Once you know the driving force, you can begin to rehearse a better way to act. This will be your antidote should the situation arise again. A word of warning here: be sure you are not replacing one negative way of acting with another. We are not rearranging the furniture here; we are having a clear out, exchanging our old furniture for new.

After some time you will become more skilled at spotting unhelpful thoughts, feelings and emotions as they arise. You will then be able to implement the antidote before you do an unhelpful act. But this takes time, so for now use the daily review to look back over the day and see what worked well and what didn't. What we are trying to do is embrace the things that worked and leave the things that didn't work by replacing them with helpful ones.

Another word of warning: do not identify with the negative thoughts, feelings and emotions. Don't think, 'I am unhappy' or

'I am depressed'. Think along the lines of, 'There is unhappiness' or 'There is depression'. If we personalise what is going on, it will be extremely hard for us to let it be or try another strategy.

So if we want change, we must look at our thoughts and the feelings, emotions and actions that stem from them. Do not underestimate the power of your mind. The mind is extremely good at gathering, storing and analysing information. It then uses this information at a later date. This means the mind is conditioned by the past, and so it will always try to re-create what it knows and is familiar with, even if it is painful. This means we are always operating from outdated concepts and beliefs that make our lives an elaborate illusion.

Because the mind is conditioned, it follows that our thoughts stem from old habits, training and social conditioning. We actually believe we are creating new possibilities, but when we take the time to watch our thoughts, we find we are just recycling old patterns that have been learned from teachers, religions, parents, friends, society and so on. The thought may have passed its sell-by date and is no longer serving us, but if we don't stop and look, we will not be able to change the harmful ones or reinforce the helpful ones. We will just continue to blindly follow them. This is one reason why people who have an addiction keep repeating their destructive behaviour. Their mind is conditioned and it just re-creates what is familiar and, for them, safe.

It seems we do not give much importance to our thoughts. We tend to attach the most importance to physical actions, less to speech, and least of all to our mental actions. Beating a person seems to us a more serious action than speaking to him insultingly, and both seem more serious than the ill will we have toward that person.

This is the wrong way round. The most important is our thoughts because, as I have stated above, our actions spring from them. It doesn't matter how many mantras you recite; how many prostrations you do; where you go on a pilgrimage; what so-called higher practice you follow; what language you chant your prayers in; or who your teacher is—if you haven't become fully aware of your thoughts, these practices are not going to give you the change you desire. That change can come about only when we become aware of what thoughts are arising, and how we deal with these thoughts.

So this is why it is important for us to become aware of our thoughts. In this way we can start to weed out the negative ones and plant positive ones. It isn't easy because our mind is lazy and will constantly try to return to its default mode, which it feels comfortable with. However, we have to persevere and bring it out of its comfort zone. This can sometimes be painful, but stick with it as it is going to be worth it in the end.

As it can be painful sometimes, you should be gentle with yourself. This daily review is here to help you, so do not push yourself too hard. Work slowly, as you will not be able to change everything at once. The things that drive us have built up over the years, in fact since the moment we were born, so they are not going to loosen their grip instantly. Look upon yourself as a tree that is deeply rooted in the ground and be patient. Training the mind is similar to potty training a baby. You constantly have to keep showing it a better way to act.

7

What's Your View?

In the fourth of Gautama Buddha's truths he explains the path we need to take to free ourselves from suffering. It is known as the eightfold path and it comprises of three aspects:

Seeing Clearly

- Appropriate View
- Appropriate Intention

Living Responsibly

- Appropriate Speech
- Appropriate Action
- Appropriate Livelihood

Staying Focused

- Appropriate Effort
- Appropriate Mindfulness
- Appropriate Concentration

Over the next few postings I will cover all of these eight points.

Appropriate View – setting off on the eightfold path without the appropriate view is like starting a journey without a map. If you get into your car without knowing where you're going and what landmarks you will encounter along the way, you are bound to get lost. Similarly, if you set off on this path and have no idea what you are doing, you will also become lost and disillusioned. First get the view correct, and the rest of the path will become clearer. You will be able to dispel any confusion or misunderstandings, and have a better understanding of reality.

We need to understand the four noble truths and the workings of cause and effect. This is the appropriate view.

When we understand the four noble truths, we will also understand that the causes of our suffering lie within our own minds, we will then realise that nirvana, the escape from suffering, also lies within our minds. Once we know this we will want to look for the causes of this suffering, which are the three poisons; attachment, anger and unawareness. Finally, having understood that life is suffering, we will be ready to set off along the eightfold path.

We should also ensure we have an understanding of cause and effect. Here some would say we actually need to understand the workings of karma, but this is such a hot potato these days.

If you believe in karma and rebirth, and it motivates you to be a good person, then follow that view. However, if you are not a lover of rebirth and prefer to keep your Buddhism firmly planted in this life, then you should understand cause and effect.

Whatever we do there will be a result. If we kill someone, we will be punished. If we lie and cheat people, we will be disliked. If we are unwilling to help people, they will not want to help us when we need it. If we are a kind, caring and compassionate person, people will be drawn to us. If we are generous, we will get back far more than we give – here I am not talking in monetary terms, but in the wonderful satisfaction of helping others.

Life is like an echo. Whatever you put out comes back. Whatever you sow, you will reap. Whatever you give, you will get. Whatever we do will always come back to us. This is not some metaphysical dogma, just plain common-sense. It is the way life is.

So by understanding cause and effect we will be driven to act in a kind and compassionate way. If you understand it and still decide to act in an unhelpful way, you will only have yourself to blame when things don't go right for you.

Once you have the appropriate view concerning suffering and cause and effect, you will be ready to move along the path.

8

The Spark That Fires Us into Action

The second aspect of the eightfold path is appropriate intention. Here I am talking about our motivation; the spark that fires us into action.

Appropriate intention is divided into three parts: letting go, goodwill and harmlessness. So let's look at these one by one.

Letting go – what we are letting go of is attachment to, or craving for, objects of desire. How much we let go is a personal thing, but the more we loosen our grip on objects of desire, the less we suffer, because Gautama Buddha stated that clinging to desire is one of the causes of our suffering. Until we are able to let go of this craving, we will never reach a place where there is no more suffering.

Letting go of our clinging desires may sound easy, but when we try to release our grip on cherished objects, a strong feeling inside tries to stop us from succeeding. This is because since time immemorial, we have been attached to our friends, family and belongings. Thus, it is never easy to suddenly let go. It may not be easy, but it isn't impossible.

Gautama Buddha taught us that letting go isn't about giving up all material things but secretly still cherishing them. What he said is that by understanding the nature of desire, we manage to let go of our cravings. We must investigate our desires and understand their true nature: impermanence and suffering.

If we contemplate impermanence we will see that nothing lasts forever. So what is the point of getting ourselves worked up over something that isn't exactly what we think it is, and isn't going to last. We will never be able to find permanent happiness from impermanent things.

So contemplating impermanence is one of the best ways of letting go of clinging to objects of desire. It takes time to change our perceptions and it isn't easy, but if we don't start, we will never finish.

A wise person is able to let go.
To let go is actually to receive,
to receive boundless happiness.

Goodwill – this is the opposite of ill-will and is a mental state. When we have goodwill towards others, we wish them well and do not want any harm to befall them. However, it is too easy for us to start wishing ill-will on others. Let's look at some examples.

If you have just separated from your partner and it all ended a bit messy, you may wish that your partner comes to some harm. This is ill-will, and such thinking is only going to bring harm upon yourself. First, we think and then we act. So if our thoughts are negative, it follows that our actions are also going to be negative.

Another example would be if you are in line for promotion and the only thing in your way is your colleague. Out of jealousy and pride, you wish that some harm befalls your colleague, so you could get the promotion. This is nothing but ill-will and based on your own selfish needs; it does not show any regard for the other's thoughts and feelings.

We want happiness in our lives, but we must understand that every other person also wants happiness. How, then, do we liberate ourselves from ill-will? The thought that other people also seek happiness causes goodwill to rise within us and makes us wish that they be happy, peaceful and well. In other words caring for others' feelings and showing them genuine warmth clears away ill-will.

I am not talking about sympathy or pity, but real empathy – putting ourselves in other people's shoes and truly understanding that they wish to be treated kindly and with warmth.

One of the best methods of building goodwill is to do the Metta-Bhavana meditation.

Harmlessness – this is the intention to not hurt anyone, either physically, mentally or verbally. We have to realise that we are not the only ones suffering. Everyone wishes to be free of suffering but is still gripped by pain, despair, anguish, dissatisfaction and other kinds of suffering.

We must understand that we, too, play our parts in other people's suffering by not having compassion for them, not caring for their well-being and not seeing that, like us, they want to be free of all types of suffering.

So how do we begin to feel compassion towards everyone? We have to contemplate on people's suffering, but don't just pick people you know and like. Also contemplate on people you dislike and don't know. Think of how people are suffering and radiate compassion towards them. This, of course, will not stop their suffering, but it will make you a more compassionate and helpful person.

We have to ensure that whatever we think, say or do does not harm anyone – this is the intention of harmlessness.

(You can find a compassion guided meditation practice here: **www.buddhismguide.org/guided-meditations/**)

9

The Power of Speech

Speech is a very powerful tool. If we hit someone, it will hurt for a short time and then go away. But if we verbally attack someone, those words can stay with them for many years. On the other hand, well thought out words can stop conflict, make friends and heal rifts. This is the power of speech and this is why Gautama Buddha included appropriate speech in the eightfold path.

Appropriate speech can be divided into four parts, namely refrain from lying, refrain from divisive speech, refrain from harsh words and refrain from gossiping.

When we tell lies it is obviously going to hurt and mislead others, but it will also harm ourselves. Nobody likes a liar, and once you get the reputation, it is difficult to lose it. Whenever you tell people things they will not believe you, even if it is true. They will try to avoid you and you will find it difficult to make friends. This will of course make you angry and frustrated, but you will only have yourself to blame.

There is a bigger picture here too, as lying can affect the whole of society, especially if the lie comes from a person of responsibility and trust. I am thinking here of politicians. There are not many people in the world these days that fully trust their politicians. You hear people say that they only voted for this particular politician because he is the best of a bad bunch. The reason for this is because they have told so many lies over the years that trust has been lost.

We must remember that we do not like to be lied to, so don't lie to others. This will free your mind of any guilt and leave it more peaceful.

Divisive speech refers to speech that is intended to create a rift or division between people. It is used to alienate one person or a group from another.

People generally do such things when driven by hatred of a person, or to win affection for themselves, or if they are jealous of someone else's success, or even out of some perverse pleasure of seeing someone fall from grace.

You can see this type of speech in all walks of life, but it is more prominent within groups and in the work place.

What is the antidote to divisive speech? It is speech that promotes friendship and harmony, speech based on kindness and compassion, which wins the trust and affection of others.

Harsh words are usually born out of anger and cause harm and pain to the hearer. Swear words, bitter words spoken in anger, words used for scolding someone, or words that belittle the hearer or someone close to them are all examples of harsh words. They are designed to take away a person's dignity.

Harsh words may make you feel good temporarily but the receiver will feel downhearted. These words are usually spoken in the spur of the moment, and so are not as severe as words which are premeditated.

There are several antidotes to harsh words, but the most important one is patience. If we are patient and respect other people's shortcomings, and do not react to others' criticism, if we bear abuse without the urge to retaliate, and respect others' viewpoints, we will not feel the need to let loose a barrage of abusive words.

Gossiping, or idle speech, is shallow and pointless. It is a form of communication that adds absolutely no value to anyone's lives. It stems from the three poisons; desire, anger and unawareness. All it does is stir up everyone's emotions and lead to negative feelings between all parties.

To counter this, which is not easy, you should watch what you say, when you say it and to whom. You should think before you speak.

I believe to ensure we have appropriate speech we should ask our self the following questions: Is what I am going to say useful? Is it going to hurt someone? Is my speech motivated by desire, anger or unawareness? Would I like other people to say the same things to me?

If we check our speech before we open our mouths, we will never speak words that do harm. Sometimes it is more powerful to say nothing at all.

Before I finish, I just want to say something about the written word. In Gautama Buddha's day this was not a problem, so he didn't mention the appropriate written word, but today it is becoming a problem.

The written words I'm talking about are newspapers, magazines, the internet and social networking sites, such as Twitter and Facebook. Obviously, freedom of speech is a human right, but if your written words are going to harm others or stir up trouble they should not be written.

If you are going to write something down you should check your motivation. Is it going to be productive and helpful, or is it going to harm or waste the readers' time?

10

Appropriate Action

The next part of the eightfold path is appropriate action. This is talking about actions of the body. We have to ensure that our actions do not bring harm to ourselves and others. One way of doing this is by refraining from the ten unwholesome ways to act. They are as follows:

- Refrain from taking the life of any being
- Refrain from taking what is not freely given
- Refrain from inappropriate sexual conduct
- Refrain from lying
- Refrain from divisive speech
- Refrain from using harsh words
- Refrain from idle talk (gossip)
- Refrain from coveting other's possessions and positions
- Refrain from resenting the good fortune of others
- Refrain from holding a closed mind about things one doesn't fully understand

If we refrain from these ten we will not be harming others with our body, speech or mind. Gautama Buddha divided appropriate action into three parts; refrain from taking life, refrain from stealing and refrain from inappropriate sexual misconduct.

Refraining from taking life, or causing others to take life, is not just talking about humans but all beings. It is no good us refraining from taking life if we encourage or pay for others to take life. Gautama Buddha taught that all life is precious and so it should not be ended by others.

It should be noted here that I am talking about intentionally taking life. It is of course a fact of life that we unintentionally kill things every time we walk around. If we walk across a field to meet a friend, we take the lives of many insects. However, this is not our intention; we just wanted to meet someone. If we are present in the moment and conscious of every step, we can reduce the lives we take and the harm we cause.

We may feel that taking the lives of flies or mosquitoes don't count, but of course they do. Every being is interconnected and so by killing something we are somehow tipping the balance of nature. So to live in harmony with the world, we must refrain from killing.

When we take something that has not been given, we are hurting ourselves as well as others. Obviously, people will be upset and hurt if you steal from them, but you will also get yourself a bad reputation. People will not trust you or want you as a friend, which will upset and hurt you.

Gautama Buddha was not just talking about stealing here, but also fraud, deceit and cheating people out of money. All of these acts are carried out due to greed, jealousy, pride and sometimes even hatred.

The way to counter this is by having respect for other people's belongings, being honest, generous and, above all, contented with what we have.

If we are honest, we would never steal or defraud anyone. If we act out of generosity, we would not want anybody else's possessions; in fact we would want to share our own belongings and wealth.

If we are content, and this really is the heart of the matter, we would see no need to take what does not belong to us, or cheat another person in any way, because we would already have enough to keep us satisfied.

Inappropriate sexual conduct is when we cause harm to someone with the sexual act. This includes rape, forcing your partner to have sex when they do not want to and having sex with an under-age child. All of these will bring harm to them and so we must refrain from these acts.

If we do not kill, do not steal and do not use sex in an inappropriate way, we will not be causing harm to anyone and we will be following Gautama Buddha's appropriate action.

11

An Appropriate Livelihood

An appropriate livelihood is one that does not bring harm to anyone or anything. Gautama Buddha listed five professions that constitute wrong livelihoods. They are dealing in weapons, dealing in humans, dealing in meat production, dealing in intoxicants and dealing in poisons.

Traditionally these professions are dismissed out of hand, but I feel a little uncomfortable with that. I have Indian friends that have joined the army so they can provide for their parents and siblings. They didn't go in to the army with the sole intention of killing people, although that may be a consequence of their action. Also, if a country didn't have an army, how long would it be before another country took it over? In addition, in today's world the army also does peacekeeping missions and so, in that way, is actually helping society.

It is clear that it isn't as black and white as Gautama Buddha's list suggests. I think one should aim for a profession that does not harm, is not deceitful and dishonest, and doesn't involve trickery, treachery or any kind of fortune-telling.

Gautama Buddha went into a lot of detail regarding the last one, fortune-telling, in the Samannaphala Sutra:

Whereas some priests and contemplatives, living off food given in faith, maintain themselves by wrong livelihood, by such lowly arts as:

reading marks on the limbs [e.g., palmistry];

reading omens and signs;

interpreting celestial events [falling stars, comets]; interpreting dreams;

reading marks on the body [e.g., phrenology];

reading marks on cloth gnawed by mice;

offering fire oblations, oblations from a ladle, oblations of husks, rice powder, rice grains, ghee, and oil; offering oblations from the mouth;

offering blood-sacrifices;

making predictions based on the fingertips;

geomancy;

laying demons in a cemetery;

placing spells on spirits;

reciting house-protection charms;

snake charming, poison-lore, scorpion-lore, rat-lore, bird-lore, crow-lore;

fortune-telling based on visions;

giving protective charms;

interpreting the calls of birds and animals ...

[The list goes on and on but I think you get the point]

Translated from Pali by Thanissaro Bhikkhu.

Any type of fortune-telling or predicting the future is a form of deceit and trickery, even if it is done by some religious person. I believe all you are doing is peddling false hope.

It is never right to deal in humans, such as prostitution, people trafficking, forcing children into work or teaching them to fire a weapon. Nor is it right to make illegal drugs and poisons. All of these professions are bringing harm to people and so should be avoided.

The bottom line is that our livelihood must not bring harm to people, animals or the environment. If we stick to this we will be on the road to living a responsible life.

12

Life Takes Great Effort

Gautama Buddha has shown us a path; it is up to us to follow it. However, our minds have a tendency to hop and jump around like a drunken frog.

We need to stay firmly focused on the job at hand. Without effort or focus, it is so easy to get distracted or drawn back into habits or activities that lead us away from the spiritual path or indeed, from leading a responsible life. Life teaches us that in order to achieve anything, we need to exert effort. We learn this at school during exams, at work when going for a promotion, or simply while trying to maintain good relations with the people around us. The eightfold path is no different. As the famous saying goes, 'No pain, no gain'. Although what would be more apt in this case is: 'No effort, no gain.'

Our minds are defiled by desire, anger and ignorance, and we need to transform them into liberated minds, free of desire, anger and ignorance, at peace, at ease. This can only be achieved by the consistent application of appropriate effort. This is aided by following Gautama Buddha's guidance on living responsibly. But even responsible living cannot be achieved without effort and focus. Let's look at some examples.

At the end of the day, you sit and do your daily review. You realise that you have spent a good part of the day gossip-mongering. You feel regret, and realise that you have wasted your time. What is to be done then? You must start to apply the antidote right there and then. It is no good trying to stop yourself from gossiping once you are already immersed in idle conversation. The effort has to be applied beforehand. You must cultivate kindness and compassion for others. You have to replace the habit of gossiping with the habit of compassion towards the person about whom you have been spreading idle talk. It is a slow process and will take a lot of effort, but slowly you will be able to stop getting involved with gossip, because you will understand that the person you are talking about does not want to suffer and only craves happiness, like yourself.

Another example would be attachment to sense objects, for example, the latest gadget like the iPhone. Your interest is first aroused by an advertisement in a newspaper. You then search the Internet for some product reviews and your excitement grows. Your anticipation is high. The product arrives in the shops and the shopkeeper gives you a call. One hour later it's in your hands and you are playing with it. The more you look at it, the more you see how indispensable it is, and you get convinced that it is the one thing that can bring you true happiness in life. You can't think of anything else, and spend the next few weeks proudly showing it to your friends, who will likely envy you for having it. Every time you look at it, a warm feeling fills you. You are so happy – your life seems complete. Then the inevitable happens – a newer, faster, smaller and more powerful version comes out. You hold the iPhone in your hand, but your happiness has turned to discontentment. Why is that? Gautama Buddha taught us that all sense objects, including those fashionable technical gadgets, are impermanent. There is no happiness inherent in them; we simply project happiness onto these objects.

In *A Guide to the Bodhisattva's Way of Life,* Shantideva said that sense objects are like honey smeared upon a razor's edge. To see this clearly, we need to train our minds to see the impermanent and unsatisfactory nature of sense objects in our everyday lives. By first being aware when some attachment or attraction occurs in our experience. Instead of getting carried away by this desire and strengthening it, we can instead analyse it and contemplate the true nature of this object. This is a slow process and takes a lot of effort, but slowly you will become accustomed to this line of thought, which will start to act as an antidote to your craving desire. The point is not necessarily to completely remove the desire for sense objects, but to loosen the grip they have on us and to be more realistic about their nature.

By acting in this way, we will be putting in the appropriate effort and will transform our unhelpful actions into helpful ones.

13

Mindfulness.....The Bottom-line

What do we need to be mindful of? Everything. We have to be mindful of our actions and the impact they have on ourselves and others. These actions will shape our lives now and in the future, and it is very important to be constantly mindful.

We have to be aware of our speech, of what we are saying. We have to be mindful of our body actions and again, be aware of their impact. We have to be mindful of our thoughts, feelings and emotions. We also have to be mindful of the work we do and its impact on society. We have to be mindful of the effort we are putting into ensuring all of our actions of body, speech and mind are in line with living responsibly.

Mindfulness is not a process of doing something, rather it is a matter of doing nothing – not judging, not thinking, not planning, not wishing, not imagining. All of these are just interferences, things the mind does to take control. But mindfulness is just watching and letting go. In this process, there is no need to cling to anything. Thus, the mind stays anchored in the present and does not float back to the past with all its memories, or to the future with its hopes and fears.

Gautama Buddha stated in the Digha Nikaya, and various other sutras, that there are Four Foundations of Mindfulness:

- Mindfulness of body
- Mindfulness of feelings
- Mindfulness of mind
- Mindfulness of mental qualities

Mindfulness of Body means being aware of your body and all the actions carried out by it. There are many different ways of contemplating the body, but a simple and effective one is doing a full body review.

Sit on a cushion with your legs crossed and back straight. Start by concentrating on your toes. Are they relaxed or tense? If they are tense, just relax them and release the tension. Now move to your feet and do the same. Do not spend more than 6 seconds on each area, or you run the risk of becoming fixated on a certain part of the body. Slowly move up your body, watching where the tension is and releasing it. In today's world, we always seem to be running from pillar to post, so this meditation will help you get back in tune with your body. I am sure you will be surprised at how much tension you are carrying around in your body.

(You can find a body scan guided meditation practice here: **www.buddhismguide.org/guided-meditations/**)

What does mindfulness of body mean on an everyday basis? It means that whatever you do with your body affects you and everyone around you. When you live responsibly, you have to be mindful of the unwholesome acts you do with your body – stealing, sexual misconduct and killing. You should look back on the day and see what actions you have carried out with your body. The ones that are conducive to responsible living should be noted. This will ensure that, with enough repetition, they soon become spontaneous. The ones that are not conducive to living responsibly should also be noted and a clear effort should be made to not do them again. This can be done by rehearsing a better way to have acted, so in the future you will naturally act in a different way. It is through staying mindful of the actions of our bodies that we will be able to live responsibly.

Mindfulness of Feelings There are three types of feelings: pleasant, unpleasant and neutral. One of these three is present during every moment of our experience. They may be strong or weak, clear or cloudy, but they are always present.

If we are not mindful and leave our feelings unchecked, pleasant feelings can lead to desire, painful feelings to hatred and neutral feelings to ignorance.

A good time to check your feelings is during your daily review session. When you think of an incident that happened that day, check to see what feelings it invoked in you. Did it bring up pleasant, painful or neutral feelings? Don't try and control or judge the feelings, just be mindful of them and then let them go.

Mindfulness of Mind is looking at the mind as though you are looking in a mirror. Ask yourself, 'How is my mind at the moment?' 'Is it full of desire, full of anger, full of ignorance; is it present in the moment or distracted?' We should look at our mind in this way, and just see it as it is, not pass any judgement or think of it as 'my mind'. We have to turn the mind upon itself and see if it is associated with any of the ten unwholesome states. If it is, do not cling to that, simply note it and let it pass.

Our minds, if left unchecked, can lead us into all kinds of situations. This is why Gautama Buddha stated that we should observe our minds, but not engage with what we see – just let it go.

We rarely stop and spend time on observing our minds. We just let thoughts, hopes, fears and dreams come and go unchecked. During your daily review session, observe your mind and see what state it is in: is it tired, lazy, angry, happy or disturbed? Note the state, but don't try to change it. Awareness of our mind will help us lead a life where we are not getting disturbed nor disturbing others.

In *A Guide to the Bodhisattva Way of Life* , Shantideva says:

Whenever I have the desire
To move my body or to say something,
First of all I should examine my mind
And then, with steadiness, act in a proper way.

Mindfulness of Mental States When we begin to be mindful of mental states, we start to see obstacles arise in the form of the five hindrances. These hindrances are mental states that can lead us astray, take us away from responsible living. The hindrances are – being gripped by desire, feelings of ill will, lack of interest, restlessness and doubt.

It would be safe to say that we have all had days when we feel lazy or anxious, and unable to stay focused. There are other days where we are so consumed by our desires, we cannot think of anything else. Maybe someone upset us the previous day and due to our thoughts of ill will, we are unable to focus. Of course, there is doubt, too. If we carry around this strong feeling of uncertainty or disbelief, it is very difficult for us to concentrate. During your daily review, look at what hindrances have distracted you recently. There is a lot of ground to cover here, so maybe it is best for you to concentrate one week on mind and mental states, another week on body, and finally a week on speech. If you do this review, you will see that the hindrances that occur on a regular basis. It is the antidotes to these hindrances you have to concentrate on and be mindful of. Apply whatever antidotes are required to remove your frequent hindrances.

This brings us to the end of appropriate mindfulness. If we are going to be mindful, and live a responsible life, we have to be fully aware of, but not tangled up in, our bodies, feelings, minds and mental states. By being mindful, we will be able to take full responsibility for all our actions. This will ensure that our minds become calmer and we travel through life in the present moment, not being tossed backwards and forwards from past to future. Being mindful means being conscious of every thought, feeling, emotion and action.

14

Something to Meditate On

Traditionally, what is talked about in appropriate meditation is being able to concentrate single-mindedly on an object of meditation. However, I feel that before we can get to that point, we need to learn about single-minded concentration on our actions of body, speech and mind – our daily actions, in other words. How do we do this? We study Buddhist teachings, contemplate them and then meditate on them.

If we meditate, we make the teachings a part of our lives. We are able to bring them into every aspect of our lives. It also allows us to move beyond mere intellectual understanding to make the teachings our own. When we read books or hear teachings, we understand them on an intellectual level. This is knowledge, but we have to turn that knowledge into wisdom. The way to do that is to meditate.

Padmasambhava told his disciple, Yeshe Tsogyal, in an oral instruction: 'It is of no benefit to know about the Dharma (Gautama Buddha's teachings). You must take it to heart and put it into practice.'

The way to live a responsible life is to meditate on the eightfold path. Make it a part of our lives and we can check our progress everyday at a daily review session.

While meditating on appropriate view, you have to really understand the workings of karma. You have to realise that whatever intentional actions you do – be it with your body, speech or mind – they will create a reaction in the future. You need to meditate on this point, so that it becomes more than just intellectual information. You have to be naturally aware of it whenever you perform any intentional action.

You also have to study the impermanence of all phenomena, and the non-existence of a true self. These two points should be studied with a teacher, as they are quite profound. You should contemplate them and ask questions to dispel any doubts you may have. Finally, you have to meditate on them.

After that, you should meditate on appropriate intention. You should not harm others, nor have ill will towards them, and your actions should not be driven by any of the three poisons. All of our actions stem from our mind and so it is only we who can be held responsible for them. You must contemplate on your every action. In this way you will not be intentionally disturbing yourself or others.

Next, meditate on appropriate speech. Many a time, we open our mouths before engaging our brains, and what comes out is harmful and unhelpful words. We lie, commit slander, use harsh words and gossip with such ease, it is frightening. It is as if our mouth has a life of its own. How do you address this problem? It's simple, meditate on your speech.

Lying is never going to help anyone. We may say we lied so as not to upset someone, but when they find out we have lied, they get more upset. When we slander someone, we are not making friends but enemies. Swearing in someone's face is going to hurt them, and gossiping is a waste of time. Thus you have to meditate on how you speak and only then will you learn to talk in a way that is both helpful and kind.

Now, appropriate action. As Gautama Buddha advised his son, Rahula:

> 'If there is a deed you wish to do, reflect this way: is this deed conducive to my harm, or to the harm of others or to both? Then this is a bad deed entailing suffering. Such a deed must be resisted.
>
> If there is a deed you wish to do, reflect this way: is this deed not conducive to my harm, or to the harm of others or to both? Then this is a good deed entailing happiness. Such a deed you must do again and again.'

Thus, we must ensure we are fully in-tune with our actions, so that we are aware of when we are being led astray by the three poisons.

This brings us to appropriate livelihood. Again, ensure that your work does not harm anybody and bring suffering to them. Think about your chosen profession, and if you see that you are harming a living being, try to change jobs, or at the very least minimise the damage you cause. Here, we have to not only meditate on our livelihood, but we also have to be honest about the effect we are having on the world.

In all of the above ensure you put in the appropriate effort and appropriate mindfulness, because it is impossible to sit quietly and mentally still on the meditation cushion if you are not at ease. If our minds are agitated by hatred, consumed with jealousy, being held by desire and greed, if we are killing, stealing and lying, how can we sit and meditate peacefully and productively? This is why you need to study the eightfold path, contemplate it, meditate on it, implement it and finally you will be able to live responsibly.

Let us try to put appropriate meditation in a nutshell. When our minds are unguarded and we are not concentrating, our actions, speech and thoughts are also unguarded. On the other hand, when our mind is concentrating, mindful and guarded, our actions, speech and thoughts are also guarded. According to Shantideva in *A Guide to the Bodhisattva Way of Life*:

> O you who wish to guard your minds,
> I beseech you with folded hands:
> Always exert your selves to guard
> Mindfulness and alertness!

15

Separating Love from Attachment

Gautama Buddha stated attachment to loved ones are causing us to suffer. When some people hear this they say things like, 'so I can't love my family, friends or children?' They say this because they are getting attachment and love confused. They really are not the same thing.

Of course we should love and have compassion for our families and friends; in fact we should love and have compassion for everyone. Gautama Buddha wasn't cold-hearted or a killjoy, he was stating a fact of life, holding onto people causes us endless suffering. Love people, for sure, but what we shouldn't do is hold onto them as though they belong to us and they are going to be around forever. It is this holding on tightly, and thinking people are permanent, that is causing us to suffer.

We think this person is mine and I will always have them. So when they die, leave us or simply stop caring for us we are not mentally prepared for it and we invariably suffer. This is attachment, it is not love.

If we understand that things change and nothing lasts forever, we will be able to love without attachment, and in my eyes that is true love. Enjoy the people around you at the moment, but keep in mind that someday they will not be there. This is love.

If you are still struggling to see the difference between love and attachment, this story may help. One day you are walking through a forest and you come upon a beautiful, fragrant flower. You stand there and admire it for some time. It fills your heart with such joy and wonderment. If you leave the flower there for others to enjoy, this is love. If you pick the flower and take it home for you to look at, this is attachment.

There is a fine line between love and attachment, but if you can separate the two, you will be able to cherish the people around you without causing them or you any type of suffering.

16

Four Thoughts to Contemplate

How can we make our life more meaningful and live it responsibly? One way is to start each day by reciting and contemplating the following points:

1. My life is special and so I should cherish it and use it to help others. If I cannot help, I should at least not harm anyone.
2. All of my happiness and suffering are impermanent, so I won't hold on to them as though they are everlasting.
3. My actions have consequences, not in another life, but here in this life. So I should act skilfully by being mindful of my actions of body, speech and mind.
4. My attachment to this life brings me discontentment. So I should try to let go and see life as an every-changing thing.

I believe by spending 10 minutes a day on contemplating each of these points, you will start to live a more enjoyable and responsible life. The best time to contemplate these points is in the morning before you start your day. This will ensure your day gets off to a good start and your mind is in a positive place.

These points are not religious or dogmatic in anyway, so you don't have to be a Buddhist, or even religious, to make these contemplation's a part of your daily routine.

Try them; I am sure you will be inspired!

17

Misunderstanding Buddhism

There is a 12-year-old boy in the village where I live and he spends the day begging. It isn't his fault because he, along with his mentally challenged mother, have been thrown out of their home by the father. I am extremely concerned about this little guy, and one day last week I was discussing what can be done to help him with two friends of mine. A Buddhist monk joined us and I explained my concerns to him. He simply said, 'It's his karma and he must have been bad in his past life.' He just dismissed the situation like that and started talking about something else.

This is the danger of misunderstanding or misinterpreting the words of Gautama Buddha. If you cover Gautama Buddha's words with mysticism, superstitions, elaborate ritual practices and dogma you can totally miss his point.

Firstly, he never said everything is karma and, secondly, even if he did, he wouldn't have wanted you to not help others who are suffering – remember that little thing called compassion?

My understanding of karma is that our actions have consequences. If we are a good person and ensure we do not harm others, our mind will be calm and peaceful. But if we act in a bad way and harm people, our mind will be tormented and agitated. So, if we help others we are also helping ourselves, and if we have been bad in the past we can change that and become good. So to dismiss someone's suffering by saying it is their karma is not only wrong, it's cruel.

It doesn't matter if you are a traditional Buddhist, born Buddhist or a secular Buddhist, but it does matter if you hide behind some Buddhist teaching and refuse to help a fellow human being. We must approach the teachings with a critical mind. Don't just blindly believe because it is in an ancient book or your teacher told you. Think for yourself. Does it fit in with your experience? If not, I suggest you leave it, but if it does then embrace it.

We don't know if we have been here before or if we will come back again, but what we do know is that we are here now. So we must try to minimise our own suffering and the suffering of others. We should see compassion as a verb and not just a noun we use in our prayers or meditation practice.

How would you feel if you hit on hard times and no one was willing to help you, because what you're going through is just your karma? I am sure you would be very unhappy. So please, contemplate the words of Gautama Buddha and build true compassion for yourself and others.

18

A Critical Mind

Carefully studying the sentences word by word, one should trace them in the discourse and verify them by the discipline. If they are neither traceable in the discourses nor verifiable by the discipline, one must conclude this; 'certainly, this is not the blessed one's utterance; this has been misunderstood by the bhikkhu, or by that community, or by those elders, or by that elder.' In that way, you should reject it.

This quote, taken from the Mahaparinibbana Sutra, makes it clear that we should not blindly believe what we hear, read or are told. We must test the words. If we are unable to find them in the Gautama Buddha's discourses or in his set of rules, they more than likely have been added by someone along the way.

The problem with blindly following what you are told, or have read, is that you are liable to get yourself tangled up in some mystical story and miss what Gautama Buddha actually taught. Now, there is nothing wrong with stories, as long as you can extract the point from the story and not just believe the words to be true. This is where critical thinking comes in. If we test the words against Gautama Buddha's discourses and our own experiences, we should be able to follow the Buddhist path.

However, if you just believe what a teacher has told you, or you have read, you may set off down the wrong path, get disillusioned and end up with more suffering. If you believe what elders have told you, without checking, you could get totally wrapped up in superstitions and old wives tales. Again, this is going to lead you down the wrong path and you may start thinking of Gautama Buddha as a god – which he clearly wasn't.

Let's expand on this point. When Gautama Buddha was asked if he was a god or a celestial being he stated that he was not, but he was awakened. Now, if you read some stories you could start to believe that he was a god, because they state he was born from under the arm, he walked as soon as he was born, where he placed his feet lotuses sprung up and he had many special marks on his body. So if you don't test these words against your experience and the discourses you will see him as a god.

You may wonder what is wrong with that. I believe if you see him as a god you will pray to him for help. Whereas, if you see him as a human teacher you will not expect him to do anything for you and you will in fact do the work yourself. We have to remember Buddhism is an inward journey that you have to work on yourself. So this is why seeing him as a god is a problem.

This is just one simple example, but of course there are numerous others. So, as the sutra states, carefully study the sentences word by word. If you find them not to be true, you should reject them. Remember, you must study them without approval and without scorn. This is so you are not just picking the bits you like and find easy to follow, or discarding things you find unpalatable and hard to do. That is harder than it sounds, because our nature is to try to reaffirm our beliefs.

There are many gurus or teachers who would give you different advice to this. They would insist you follow what they say and if you don't you will never reach enlightenment or whatever goal you have set yourself. I believe you should test these teachers the same way you test the written word (you should also test the words I have written here as well). If what they are saying cannot be found in the discourses or does not fit into your experiences, you should proceed with great caution. This is not easy to do if you regard your teacher as a higher being or some sort of god, but if you see them as a human being with good knowledge, it is easier to do.

Whenever you study Buddhism please do it with an open and critical mind. That way you will be on the right track.

19

Indulging in Superstitions

For centuries people have been indulging in superstitions, lucky charms, omens, divinations and fortune-telling. They have used these things to help them make decisions and keep them from taking responsibility for their own actions. Some cultures still place a lot of importance on such things. However, if you look carefully, you can see these things stem from ignorance and fear. They certainly are not a reliable way to help you navigate through life.

In Gautama Buddha's day you could put superstitions and omens down to a lack of education, but I am not sure what the reasoning is behind them in today's society. You still see people touching wood or keeping their fingers crossed to bring them good luck. Others wear a rabbit's foot for the same reason— though I think it's not very lucky for the rabbit. They don't put new shoes on a table, walk under ladders or open umbrellas in the house just in case it brings them bad luck. People become visibly scared if they break a mirror or spill salt, and don't even mention Friday the thirteenth.

In Tibetan culture it is inauspicious to start a journey on a Saturday. So people pack their things on Friday and leave the house as though they are starting their journey. But they only take their bag to a friend's house and then return home. On Saturday they collect their bag and start their journey, believing they have tricked the superstition. It is clear that this type of ignorance only creates a vicious cycle where superstitions are used to cheat other superstitions.

The list of superstitions and omens is endless, but they have one thing in common: they are totally irrational and based on fear and ignorance.

People go to fortune-tellers, psychics and gurus for divinations so they can shirk their responsibilities and get someone else to make an important decision for them. But if these people can see into the future, it would mean our lives are predetermined. That would in turn mean we could never improve our lives, as things have already been decided for us. Thankfully, this is not the case, and people who say they can see into the future are just playing on people's ignorance and fears. You may say there is no harm done, but I beg to differ. I heard of a man who was seriously ill going to a guru for a divination. He was told not to have an operation but to do some prayers instead. This person died needlessly, and painfully, because if he had had the operation, he more than likely would have survived.

There is a famous, or infamous, psychic in America, and when I was writing this blog she hit the headlines, and not in a positive way. Ten years ago a young girl went missing, and the psychic told the family she was dead and they would see her again only in heaven. It transpired that the girl wasn't dead but was being held captive for all those years. The family say the mother died of a broken heart after the psychic reading.

These two stories show just how harmful this type of trickery can be. I believe these people are acting irresponsibly and fraudulently.

Many go to holy people for blessings, believing that if they are touched on their head or they touch the feet of a guru, their lives will be OK. They also may wear something around their necks, hoping it will protect them from danger, or go to long-life ceremonies thinking that they will live a long time, even though they do not do anything to change their actions or life-style. Again, these things are just superstitions, and without you exploring your thoughts and changing your actions of body, speech and mind, you will not be able to change your life.

Gautama Buddha called all of these practices 'low art', and on many occasions he stated that such things are of no use as we have to take responsibility for our own lives. In the Anguttara Nikaya, Gautama Buddha stated that this is how responsible people act:

'They do not get carried away by superstition; they believe in deeds, aspiring to results from their own deeds through their own effort in a rational way; they are not excited by wildly rumoured superstition, talismans, omens or lucky charms; they do not aspire to results from praying for miracles'.

There is a story about a Brahman who was an expert in predictions drawn from cloth. He held a superstition that once a piece of cloth, no matter how new or expensive, was bitten by a rat, it would bring you bad luck.

On one occasion he discarded a piece of his expensive cloth in a local cemetery because he believed it had been bitten by a rat and would now bring him only bad fortune. Later on he heard that Gautama Buddha had picked up the cloth and was using it. He ran as fast as he could to find Gautama Buddha and warn him about the bad luck that was going to come his way if he didn't throw the cloth away. However, once the Brahman found him, he was dissuaded from this irrational superstition and shown that only he himself could bring good or bad circumstances into his life.

Gautama Buddha did not believe in luck, fate or chance. He taught that whatever happens does so because of a cause or causes. If you want to pass your exams, you have to study hard and put in a lot of effort. So there is a clear connection between passing the exam and study. It is of no use praying to a god, chanting a mantra or wearing some kind of lucky charm to pass your exam as there is no connection between these things.

So what did Gautama Buddha believe? He believed in individual responsibility, rational thought and social obligations rather than unhealthy fears and irrational superstitions. This point was made very clear in the Mangala Sutra. In this discourse, Gautama Buddha was asked what the most auspicious omens were and which ones should be followed. He didn't directly answer the question, but instead gave guidelines of how we can make our own lives auspicious without relying on outside omens. He spoke about thirty-eight principles that, if lived by, would bring us true protection.

These thirty-eight principles gradually lead you on a journey that will see you reforming yourself and turning into a responsible person within society. It is a practical guide that will help you find happiness and ease your suffering. It not only shows you what you need to do, but it also shows you the inevitable obstacles you will encounter whilst you travel along the path.

The thirty-eight principles in the Mangala Sutra will lead you through individual discipline, family obligations, social responsibility, and, finally, to personal development. In a nutshell: it is a guide to life.

Read about the Mangala Sutra and how you can follow the thirty-eight principles in 'Life's Meandering Path.'

20

What is Your Goal?

Recently I had an opportunity to speak to a group of Western Buddhists and I asked them why they practice and what is their end game. A good 90% of them said reaching enlightenment was why they practice. I always find it a bit disconcerting when people offer up this as a goal. I pushed them a little further and they spoke about going to a different place, such as nirvana, not being born again or residing in a Buddha field in some celestial realm. They seem to regard this place of enlightenment as a paradise full of all the nice things they like, and devoid of anything they dislike. All of which I feel is a misunderstanding of what Gautama Buddha actually wanted us to aim for. If indeed he wanted us to aim for anything at all.

I believe Gautama Buddha's main point was that life is suffering and we ourselves are the main cause of this suffering. The paths he spoke about in his teachings, such as the eightfold path, are a way for us to alleviate this suffering and live a calmer, more responsible life.

I do not believe he meant for us to dream of going to a different place, such as nirvana, paradise or heaven, once we die or to project all the things we like in this world onto these places. Heaven, nirvana and so forth are states of mind and not actual places.

Gautama Buddha never said he was enlightened. The word enlightenment is a mistranslation of the Sanskrit word bodhi, which actually means awakened.

Once Gautama Buddha was asked if he was a god, a sorcerer, a magician, angel or a celestial being and he answered no to all of these. He said he was awake. Being awake is very different to being enlightened. When we are awakened it is right here, right now, in this very life. It is being awake to or having an awareness of the way the world really is.

When he was asked to sum up his teaching in a single word, he said, "awareness." This awareness is based on our experiences and is not achieved through blindly following a teacher or some teachings. The highest authority is our own experiences. It is not enough to rely on faith or understanding Buddhism intellectually. We have to experience it as Gautama Buddha did. His teachings are all based on his own personal experiences and he strongly encouraged us to do the same.

I believe that if we want the most out of Buddhism we should keep our goals and our expectations realistic. That way we are not going to get disappointed.

21

Five Qualities of a Teacher

In the Anguttara Nikaya, Gautama Buddha stated the five qualities we should look for in a teacher:

> 'Buddist teachings should be taught with the thought, 'I will speak step-by-step'... 'I will speak explaining the sequence'... 'I will speak out of compassion'... 'I will speak not for the purpose of material reward'...'I will speak without disparaging others.'

Let's look at these five qualities, and as we go through them keep your teachers in mind and see if they embrace these five qualities.

Firstly, the teacher should speak step by step. It is of very little use to learn about emptiness or non-self, if you haven't first understood that there is an unease or discontentment running throughout your life. When I first started studying Buddhism I had so many teachings on what a Bodhisattva does and doesn't do, but didn't know exactly what I was supposed to be doing myself. I learnt about how Milarepa got enlightened in one lifetime, but Gautama Buddha took three countless aeons. I expect these stories have their place, but it certainly isn't when one is just starting out on the path. We need to start at the beginning of the path and slowly work our way along, one step at a time. This will help reduce confusion. One of the great things about Buddhism is that things are numbered – five precepts, ten harmful acts, four truths, five qualities of a teacher – and so it makes it easier to follow and remember the individual steps of the teachings.

Secondly, the teacher should explain the sequence. I have had teachings where someone has asked about why are things done in this order, only to be told that it is tradition – very annoying and not very helpful. So the sequence should be explained. Why in the four truths do we start with 'there is suffering' and then go on to 'the causes of suffering', followed by 'there is an end to suffering' and finally, 'the path that leads to the end of our suffering?' There is a reason for this sequence and your teacher should explain it clearly. This will ensure there is no confusion or misunderstanding.

Thirdly, the teacher's motivation for teaching should be one of kindness, caring and compassion. He should see that people are discontented with their lives and need some help to reduce their suffering. The teacher should not be motivated by pride, thinking they are better than their students, or arrogance, thinking they know more than their students. Their teachings should be grounded in an overwhelming sense of wanting to help others.

Fourthly, the teacher should not teach just to get material gain. In Tibetan Buddhism (and probably other forms of Buddhism as well, but I only have experience of Tibetan Buddhist teachers) many teachers have huge houses, large cars, big TV's and all the material trappings of the 21st century. This really is a turn off. How can anyone sit and listen to a teacher telling them not to get attached to things, when the teacher quite clearly is attached himself.

I do understand that some teachers are professionals and so have to charge, so as to make a living. There is no problem with that, as long as their fees are reasonable and they are not just teaching to rip people off. A friend of mine told me a story about when she went to a teaching in America. She wasn't working at the time and so had very little money, but she really wanted the teaching. She asked the centre if she could do some work for them to pay off the cost of the teaching. She was told that it wasn't a charity and she would never go to a supermarket and ask to work to pay off her grocery bill, so why is she asking here. This is wrong on so many levels.

Finally, their teachings should not disparage others. I have to be honest with you and say I have had quite a few teachings that have put other schools of Buddhism down. This, I believe, is done so the teacher can gain control over the students. They say that their teachings are the quickest, best, simplest, most powerful way to reach enlightenment – all of this is said without offering up any proof.

I have also had teachers making fun of other religions because they don't believe what Buddhists believe. One ridiculed other religions for believing in God, and then he proceeded to do a protector prayer – this prayer is to ask some mythical being outside of yourself to help you, in other words, a god.

Buddhism is just one form of help we can use to reduce our suffering. It isn't the only one. We are all different and so what suits one will not suit another. So the teacher should give you the facts and not spend time disparaging others.

I would like to add another quality that I think is also very important, and that is the five precepts. I believe any Buddhist teacher should attempt to follow the precepts. Of course they are only human and may come up short sometimes, but they should at least try to follow them. I personally find it hard to take someone seriously if they are trying to teach me how to act, when they quite clearly cannot act that way themselves. Do as I say and not as I do, doesn't wash these days.

That is how a teacher should act, but what about the student? Some people think to show respect to their teacher they have to bow down to them, treat them as higher beings, shower them with gifts and blindly follow every word they say. I do not think this sycophantic way of acting is giving respect. If you truly want to respect your teacher then listen to their teachings, ask questions to clear up any doubt, meditate on the teaching and then, finally, put what they have taught into practice. Now what better way to respect anyone?

The problem with the student acting this way is that they sometimes end up lusting after time with the teacher, hanging on their every word and doing things they wouldn't usually do, just to please this higher being. They totally forget that this is about the student, not the teacher. They project special powers onto the teacher, which they don't have. I have a friend that thinks his teacher can hear and see everything that is happening to his students. If the teacher looks at him in an angry way, he will look back over the last few days and imagine it is for something he did. This way of thinking is not just irrational, it is also dangerous, as it is leaving you wide open for abuse and a big fall.

Once you start seeing this human being as someone higher, better and more worthy than yourself, you start along that slippery slope to being taken for a ride. This is how cults are formed. You think the teacher is a god like figure and he knows what is good for you, so you surrender to him. He gets you doing irrational and quite often immoral things, but you just blindly follow, because he is the chosen one, he knows best. This can lead you to act in an unethical way, do things you would never have dreamed of doing until you met your teacher and it can also lead to psychological problems. What it definitely won't do is help alleviate your suffering.

If your teacher is any good he will tell you upfront that he does not have all the answers, he is not a higher being and he is just sharing his experiences and wants to learn from your experiences. But many teachers love the adulation, as it boosts their pride and makes them feel special. For them it is all about ego, power, control and money, it has very little to do with wanting to help others.

I think I should end on a positive note. There are without doubt some wonderful teachers out there. Ones that are compassionate, grounded and informed, we just have to root them out. I will reiterate what I said at the start of this principle, it is extremely important to have a teacher to guide us along our chosen path, so please do not be put off by bad teachers – good teachers by far outweigh the bad ones.

22

Achieving Peace and Happiness

I do not want to mislead you here, so I will say at the outset that I do not think lasting peace and true happiness are achievable. Of course, we can gain peace of mind, but as we know from experience, it isn't going to last forever – nothing is permanent and this includes peace. Happiness is a relative thing and so it is impossible to say what true happiness is and what it is not. What makes me happy will probably not make you happy and so this is why I feel true happiness is misleading.

Having said that, I do believe peace of mind and happiness is within our grasp, but they are just not permanent and so we have to continually work on them.

There are four qualities of mind that we are able to cultivate in order to reduce our suffering and become more connected with the world around us. The four states are commonly known as the four immeasurables and they are goodwill, compassion, appreciation and equanimity.

Traditionally, they are taught in the order I mentioned above. However, I believe the fourth one should come first, because if we have equanimity for all beings, it follows that we will be able to cultivate goodwill, compassion and appreciation for them.

So let's start by looking at equanimity. Our lives are full of ups and downs, and so is everyone else's. If we can face the downs as well as the ups, we will be able to cultivate an open and calm mind. It is easy to face the ups, but not so easy to come to terms with the downs, but if we don't, all we are doing is adding to our suffering.

When we look at the world we can clearly see how hard it is to obtain a balanced mind, as we are continuously in a flux of rise and falls. These lift us up one moment and fling us down the next. This is true for everyone, we are all the same. So if that is the case, why are we discriminating against others? We are all in the same boat, all riding the waves of life.

So equanimity is where we do not distinguish between our friends, the people we dislike or strangers, but regard everyone as equal.

This is not easy because when we are not being mindful we are constantly being tossed around by our prejudices and emotions. So we need to have a complete openness to our experiences, without being carried away with reactions, such as 'I like this and dislike that' or 'I love you but detest you.' A balanced mind will mean we are not going to get disturbed by the eight worldly conditions. (I will talk about these eight conditions in the next part).

What we are trying to do here is remove the boundaries between ourselves and others, by discarding our discrimination's. What we are not doing is becoming detached or feel indifferent to others. This is a common misunderstanding of what is meant by equanimity in the four immeasurables.

So we have to look upon others as our equals. See that they have their ups and downs just like us. If we can do this, equanimity will be able to grow.

What I want to do here is introduce a practice we can use while we go about our daily lives. When you feel your prejudices coming to the surface have a set phrase to mentally repeat to yourself, something like this, 'They are no different to me. They, like me, are subject to the eight worldly conditions. We are all equal.' It is better for you to have your own phrase, as it will resonate with you. By mentally repeating your set phrase you will stop your discrimination's in their track. After time we will naturally see all as equal, but that is going to take time, so for now use your set phrase.

The second immeasurable is goodwill and this is the thought that we want the best for all beings, without discriminating between the people we like and those we dislike. Sometimes our goodwill only covers people who are useful, pleasing or amusing to us. This is not how we should divide groups of people; we have to see people through the eyes of equanimity. We must open our hearts to everyone and that includes the people who make us angry, politicians from a party we disagree with, religious leaders that have different beliefs to ours, people who act and dress differently to us and those who just have the knack of rubbing us up the wrong way. All of these people deserve our goodwill and so we have to train ourselves to think only good thoughts towards them. We have to include ourselves in this. Sometimes we are harsher with ourselves than we are with others. If you can't love yourself, how are you going to love others?

If we just watch our thoughts for awhile it becomes quite apparent that this isn't how we usually think. Not every thought radiates goodwill to others, so how can we cultivate this goodwill? Here is a practice to use in your day-to-day life. I find the best antidote to judging someone, when we are not on our meditation cushion, is to have a set phrase that resonates with you, something like. 'May my mind be at ease, may you be happy, may everyone be free from suffering.' These phrases can be used when you spot ill-will arise in you.

I remember a few years ago, when I travelled to work by metro, I would see the same man every day. I didn't know anything about this man, but as soon as I saw him I would start thinking negative thoughts. It was totally irrational, and I knew that, but it just seemed to happen automatically. I spoke to my teacher at the time and he told me to try having a set phrase ready for when I encountered this man again. The next time I saw him I mentally recited my phrase and I started to see the man in a different light. After reciting my phrase for a few days I never had the negative feelings again.

The next time you start to judge someone, mentally recite your phase and the judgement will start to dissolve. Remember, we all share this planet and we all want to be happy, so the best way to end our judgmental thoughts is to wish goodwill to everyone.

Compassion, the third quality, is an understanding that the world is full of suffering and a heartfelt wish that this suffering will come to an end or at least reduce – for ourselves and others.

Some people are so wrapped up in their own world of suffering, they forget to have empathy with other people's suffering. We seem to live in a selfish world and people close their eyes and ears to the constant stream of tears. We seem to be able to watch the news or read the newspapers in a dispassionate way. The horrendous suffering that is going on throughout the world doesn't touch us. We have our own problems to deal with. This is not a kind or helpful way of thinking. If we do not have compassion for others, why should they have compassion for us? This is not the type of world we should wish to live in or leave for our children.

Through compassion the fact that everyone is suffering remains vivid in our minds. Sometimes we may feel that we are not suffering, but that should not stop us having compassion for those who are. Compassion should be ever-present. Not just for family and friends, but for everyone, even people who are acting in an unhelpful way. Once we start to discriminate who should have your compassion and who doesn't deserve it, true compassion is lost. Everyone is suffering, so everyone deserves it.

So again, have a set phrase ready to mentally recite once you feel you are not caring for another person's suffering. Something like this; 'may I be released from my suffering, may they be released from their suffering, may all beings be released from suffering, and may compassion arise in my heart.' But, as before, it is important you decide on your own wording, so it resonates with you, this is just a suggestion.

Sometimes when we are being harassed by a homeless person annoyance arises in us and not compassion, so next time that happens, mentally recite your set phrase. It doesn't mean you are going to give them all your money out of compassion, but it does mean you will feel empathy towards them. You should try to recite your phrase every time you feel that you are not being compassionate. What these phrases do is connect us to others. We appreciate that they are suffering just like us, so once we have this connection, it is easier to radiate compassion towards other beings.

I think we should see compassion as a verb and not a noun. It should be something we do and not just talk about or pray for. After spending many years going to Buddhist teachings I grew very tired of being preached to about compassion. Yet when I observed the teacher, I didn't see much evidence of it being put into action. It is beneficial to contemplate compassion, there is no doubt about that, but it is far more beneficial, for all concerned, for it to come off the cushion and out into the community.

We have to be intelligent with our compassion. It is of no benefit to give money to a drunken, homeless person. They are just going to spend it on more drink, compounding their problems. It is far better to give them food or give your money to a homeless shelter that helps these people. So compassion isn't just about giving, it's about giving sensible, and that could include money, clothing, food, your time and so on.

So in a nut shell, compassion is the humane quality of understanding the suffering of others and wanting to do something to alleviate it.

The fourth quality is appreciation. What we are appreciating is the happiness someone else is experiencing. With this quality we feel real joy at their happiness. The operative word here is real. It shouldn't be forced or faked, but real heartfelt joy. This is the perfect antidote for envy, which is a feeling of grudging admiration and desire to have something that is possessed by another. Sometimes we begrudge people their happiness and feel resentment at seeing their success. This feeling of appreciation deals a killer blow to envy.

Happiness is fleeting and so to begrudge what little joy people can find in their lives, is a very selfish and unhelpful quality. What we need to do is rejoice in what happiness comes another's way.

When I was at school I never did very well in exams, so when my friends passed their exams with flying colours, I used to feel real resentment. But who was I harming? The answer to that is myself. These negative feelings are only going to pollute one's own mind and if your mind is polluted your actions will follow in the same vein.

Later in life when I was still rubbish at passing exams, I used to think how happy my friends would feel by passing, how their parents are going to be proud and what a good future my friends were going to have. These thoughts of appreciation are far more constructive and this is what we are looking for here.

So in this quality, instead of having a set phrase ready, you should think of the joy and happiness the other person is feeling and rejoice in it. I have to say that by thinking this way a warm feeling grows in your own heart and it leaves no room for envy.

Sometimes we take joy in another's misfortune. If we radiate appreciation towards others, we will not have these awful thoughts.

Once we have a steadiness of mind, we will have thoughts of goodwill, gain compassion and appreciate the happiness others are experiencing. These are the four immeasurables. They are called immeasurables because by cultivating them we are helping to reduce the suffering of an uncountable number of people. We have to persevere with these immeasurables, so they become a natural way for us to think and not just a passing mood.

23

Worldly Conditions

Nobody's life is perfect; we all have good and bad days. This is part and parcel of worldly conditions. Sometimes the world is like a rose, all beautiful and fragrant. Other times, it is like the stem of the rose, all thorny and prickly.

An optimist will see the world as rosy, whereas a pessimist sees it as thorny. But realistically, the world is both rosy and thorny. A person who understands this point will not be seduced by the rose, or become averse to the thorns.

Gautama Buddha taught that there are eight worldly conditions and a realist will understand that the pendulum swings both ways, sometimes they will be under the sway of the four desirable conditions and sometimes the four undesirable conditions.

We have to accept that these eight worldly conditions are part of this human life. So what are the eight worldly conditions? The desirable ones are gain, status, praise and pleasure. The four undesirable being loss, obscurity, reproach and pain. It doesn't matter if we see them as desirable or undesirable, they are all causes of our suffering.

We are all subject to gain and loss, not only of material things, such as money, but also of our friends and family. We may go out and buy a new 3D television and it makes us very happy, until one day it is stolen, we then become sad – gain and loss. If you are a business man you suffer from gain and loss on a regular basis. You may have, in the past, met a wonderful person who you get on really well with, but recently they died – gain and loss. These are some examples of what we are subject to in our lives.

Status and obscurity are another two worldly conditions that confront us in the course of our daily lives. Status comes in various forms, such as celebrities and politicians, or you may be highly regarded within your profession, or even a well respected Buddhist teacher. Whatever the status, you can become attached to your public image and the prestige that goes with it. Even if we do not want to be famous, we still like to be looked upon in the best possible light. I am sure, if we are honest, we all like a bit of status, because who wants to feel unimportant or overlooked?

I am sure we have all dreamt of our fifteen minutes of fame and there is nothing wrong with that. Some people are world superstars and others are just well known in their own backyards, but whatever your status, it is important to see it as a fleeting thing. Very few people stay famous all of their lives, for most it is only a few years. So to hold on to fame as though it is something tangible is going to bring you suffering.

When we reflect on our status and obscurity, we will be able to see that they are just projections and not something solid or permanent. This releases us from the suffering they can cause.

The next two pairs of worldly conditions are praise and reproach. We all like to be told, 'Well done!' when we do something right. It makes us feel happy and gives us a sense of pride. Praise is like some sort of a drug we quite happily get addicted to. Whereas, no one enjoys being reproached, even if they have done something wrong.

If we are able to face reproach in an impassive way and remain calm even though people are saying some hurtful things about us, then we are dealing with this worldly condition in a proper way. If we give very little regard to whether we are held in high esteem or thought of as a person of no influence, then we can be said to be rising above worldly attachments.

If we are able to keep our composure when we lose out, or are glorified as being a very special, talented person, this is the sensible thing to do, even though it is not always that easy.

It is human nature to soak up praise and push away reproach. I know when someone says something nice about me I feel happy and proud, but if I am reproached I get all defensive and hurt. Through reflection on these states of mind we can understand them as one of the same; impermanent, fleeting and mere projections. This will help us let them go, and in turn, reduce our suffering.

The final pair is pleasure and pain. This is where we are the same as animals; we chase after pleasure and run away from pain. I personally do not know anyone who prefers sorrow to laughter, or harm to happiness. This is just the way we are. It is like a bond that ties us all together.

Watching pleasure and pain arising in the mind, and remaining open to them without attaching to or rejecting them, enables us to let the conditions be, even in the most emotionally charged circumstances.

I believe we all strive for pleasure and push away pain, even animals. So it is clear pleasure is what we aim for in life and not pain. But they are both things that come into being for a short time and then disappear. So in that respect they are no different. So Gautama Buddha's advice is to not welcome them or rebel against them, just let them arise and go.

When we start seeing the eight worldly conditions for what they are, and watching the mind's reaction to them, we will be able to prevent them from causing us suffering. This is not just a meditation practice, we have to take it into our day-to-day lives. We have to understand that life is full of gain, loss, status, obscurity, reproach, praise, pleasure and pain.

Someone is always going to profit and someone else will lose out; for every famous person, there are thousands of others who are unknown; if one person is reproached, another will be praised; and what gives one person pleasure, will give another pain. This is the way of the world. It doesn't matter if you are skilled in Gautama Buddha's teachings or not. You will still be subject to the eight worldly conditions. It is how you deal with these conditions that differentiate you from others.

24

Dismissing Impermanence

Recently, I was watching a short video on the last days of Mes Aynak, the ancient Buddhist site in Afghanistan that was being destroyed because it is sitting on a vast copper deposit, and I started to feel a pang of anger. I also felt like we should not just sit back and let the destruction of this site happen. I put the link on my Facebook page and shared it with as many people as possible – to what ends? I wasn't sure, but it seemed like the right thing to do.

Someone left a comment on my Facebook page saying that this is just a lesson in impermanence and we should not feel any attachment to the site. Is that true? As Buddhists should we just sit idly by and watch the world and its history being destroyed, because Gautama Buddha said everything is impermanent? I don't believe so. I think that is a misunderstanding of what he taught.

Impermanence is a great meditation practice that leads to the meditator loosening their grip on the things they are attached to. Gautama Buddha taught this practice because he realised that it is our clinging attachment to things that cause us to suffer when these things change. I believe impermanence was never meant to be a glib statement to make when a piece of the world history is about to be destroyed.

I have actually heard people say 'that's impermanence for you,' when a building has collapsed and people have died or a terrorist attack has destroyed property. Impermanence is not something to hide behind. It isn't a tool for suppressing our emotions or dismissing tragedies. Of course, we can be sad when there has been a terrorist attack, someone close to you dies or an ancient site is about to be wiped of the face of the planet. That would be a healthy way to feel. We shouldn't try to stop our emotions, just learn how to deal with them better. If anger rises in you because of an act of impermanence, find a way to let it go.

When we understand the connection between the impermanence of everything and our attachment to them, we are able to reduce some of our suffering, and this is how, I believe, Gautama Buddha meant this teaching to be understood.

Words like karma, impermanence and mindfulness are quite important words, and we should think before we use them in a dismissive way, because it leads to them being misused and misunderstood.

25

Misusing Words

The misuse of Buddhist terminology seems to be spreading, so I feel it is time to get a few things straight. Gautama Buddha taught for a reason, and that reason was to help reduce our suffering. It wasn't for us to be dismissive of what is happening around us. This is not kind, caring or compassionate. Here are some words I feel are being miss used:

Karma – this was taught to show us that our actions have consequences. Gautama Buddha wanted us to understand the principle of cause and effect. This was a way of ensuring our actions help people and not harm them. It encourages us to think before we do any actions. He did not teach so you can just dismiss something that has happened to another person. It is extremely unhelpful to tell someone it is their karma when they fall down and injure themselves.

Impermanence – this was taught to stop us getting attached to people and material objects. If we understand that things won't last, we will not get too attached to them and this will help reduce our suffering. It wasn't taught so you can smugly say to someone whose smart phone has just broken, 'that's impermanence for you.'

Samsara – this was taught so we can understand that we suffer from the moment we are born, through to old age, sickness and death. If we understand that our life has this thread of suffering running through it, we will search for the cause and the cure – this is known, in Buddhist terms, as the four truths, which Gautama Buddha decided to make his first teaching. It should be noted that samsara is a state of mind and not an actual place. He did not talk about samsara so we can use it to dismiss things that are happening in our lives and the lives of others. I have recently heard it used to brush aside climate change and what is happening to the planet.

We misuse words every day and most of the time there is no problem with that, but the misuse of these words is being carried out in an unkind and uncaring way. If you are going to use these words please first understand what Gautama Buddha was trying to convey. His teachings are a great help to us all, but when we water down his words we are causing them to lose their true value.

26

The Art of Letting Go

If you talk to some people they will tell you to just let your destructive emotions out, other people will advise you to keep them locked inside. However, Gautama Buddha stated that emotions aren't things to be dealt with, they are things to let go of. So how do we learn to let our destructive emotions go? We are all different and so what works for one, may not work for another, but for me, I learnt by doing a daily review session at the end of each day.

Before I go to sleep I sit quietly and review my day. I especially concentrate on things that haven't worked out as well as I would have expected. I start with the consequences of my action and work backwards. I look at how I acted, and what drove me to act in that way. I go all the way back to the thought, emotion or feeling that started the sequence of events off. Change is only possible once we have seen what the driving force for our action is. Let's look at an example:

The other day I got into a very heated discussion with a friend of mine about politics. I have always had a sense of fair-play and dislike it when others seem to be holding a selfish view.

This is what I believe was going on here. We were discussing Obamacare and he thought it was wrong and should be scrapped. I, of course, felt it was a great thing and was going to help thousands of people. The discussion went on for some time and we both got quite angry. It ended by him just walking away in a real rage.

So that evening I looked at the situation and traced it back to a feeling of 'I am right and you are wrong.' I was being stubborn and inflexible – neither of these is very endearing qualities. I saw that once he started to attack my views, or that is how it seemed to me, I started to get defensive. I felt the anger start to rise and saw the consequences of that anger. So I replayed the events in my head, but this time without the defensiveness and anger. The outcome was obviously more positive this time round.

Next time I am in a situation like this, I will be better prepared, because once I feel these destructive emotions start to rise, I will be able to let them go and fashion a better outcome. This takes time and a lot of effort, as we are lazy and keep going back to our comfort zone, even if it causes us to have destructive emotions – they seem familiar and safe. Training the mind is like training a small puppy to sit, you have to keep going back and pointing out a better way to act, but once you have trained your mind it is well worth the effort.

It is very important to practice moment by moment awareness, so we do not miss our destructive emotions arising. When we are not aware the emotion will rise before we have chance to let it go. So awareness is an imperative part of the process of letting go.

This review has been one of the most useful tools I have learnt and I would encourage you to try it out. It has to be done on a daily basis and not just when things have gone wrong. It is important to look at what has gone right as well, so you can reinforce your positive thoughts, feelings and emotions.

I have to impress on you that this is not a 'quick fix' solution to letting go of our destructive emotions. It really does take time, a lot of patience and constant reaffirming, but the outcome is a mind that is less tense and at peace, so it has to be worth the effort.

27

Soldiers and Buddhism

Recently, whilst teaching university students, I was asked on numerous occasions if a Buddhist can become a soldier. At first glance you would think not, because one of the five precepts states that we should refrain from killing. Also, one of the five inappropriate livelihoods says that dealing in weapons is wrong. However, Gautama Buddha seems to have made concessions on this point. In the Chakkavatti Sihanada Sutra he told a king that an army is justified as it offers protection and security for different classes of people in the kingdom from internal and external threats. In the Seeha Senapathi Sutra, he further states, whilst talking to an army officer called Seeha, he did not advise Seeha against the army or being a commander of an army, but only advised him to discharge his duties the proper way.

He did prohibit a solider from becoming a monk whilst still in military service. The story goes that his father came to him and complained that he had insulted him by begging for meals, walking house to house along the streets in his own town. He said his relatives laughed at him and they insulted him and now he was trying to destroy his father's army. It seems that many soldiers were leaving the army to become monks because they received free food and shelter. So Gautama Buddha then promulgated a law (Vinaya) stating no serving soldier can become a monk.

So I think it is clear that contrary to the popular belief, Gautama Buddha has not rejected or prohibited soldiering as a profession or occupation. He has instead recognised the necessity of an army to provide protection to the subjects of a country.

A final word on this topic. I do not want you to think Gautama Buddha thought war and killing was a good thing, he certainly did not. It states this in the Dhammapada:

Victory breeds hatred
The defeated live in pain,
Happily the peaceful live,
Giving up victory and defeat
Victory and defeat are two sides of the same coin of War.

So it isn't as black and white as the list of five precepts and inappropriate livelihoods may suggest.

28

What Does Buddhism Say About Homosexuality?

Is homosexuality forbidden in Buddhism? Is it sexual misconduct? Let's look at what Gautama Buddha and Tibetan Buddhism say.

Gautama Buddha stated in one of the five precepts that lay-people should refrain from sexual misconduct. He never really elaborated on this point, only to say that a man should not fool around with a woman that is married or betrothed. He did of course say in the Vinaya, which are the rules for monks and nuns, that they have to take a vow of celibacy, but no such rule was made for lay-people.

So he left this precept sweet and simple. In some ways this is a good thing, as I don't think holy men and religions should concern themselves with the sexual act. However, as it is so vague it does give others the chance to interpret it in a way that suits their world view and allows them to tag all of their prejudices onto it.

I personally believe that Gautama Buddha taught the five precepts to steer us away from causing harm to ourselves and others. It should be noted here that the precepts are not commandments, and are five things we should try to refrain from. If the sexual act is not going to cause harm it should be consensual, affectionate, loving and not breaking any marriage vow or commitment. It should also not be abusive, such as sex with an under-age person or rape, and this includes forcing your partner into having sex. So I believe in this way a consenting, loving homosexual act isn't in any way against Gautama Buddha's teachings.

In Tibetan Buddhism it is viewed quite differently. In fact, Dalai Lama has come out (excuse the pun) and said that from a Buddhist point of view lesbian and gay sex is considered sexual misconduct. Now he is not deriving this view from the discourses of Gautama Buddha, but from a 15th century Tibetan scholar called Tsongkhapa. Here is a brief outline of Tsongkhapa's medieval thinking:

He prohibits sex between two men, but not between two women.

He prohibits masturbation, oral and anal sex.

He does not allow sex for anyone during day light hours, but allows men five orgasms during the night.

He allows men to pay for sex from prostitutes.

He gave a full list of what orifices and organs may and may not be used, and even what time and place people can have sex (Gautama Buddha never made these distinctions).

As you can see Tsongkhapa heavily weighed the odds in men's favour – not surprising, as he was a man. In fact, it appears his list only seems to be aimed at men, in Tibetan culture women should do what men want them to do. That point comes across loud and clear when married women , who are seen to belong to their husband, have no say in whether they want sex or not. Of course, this is beginning to change with the young generation.

It would appear Tsongkhapa was trying to force lay-people to adhere to rules that were actually meant for monks and nuns. This way of thinking stems not from Buddhism but is a cultural thing.

It does seem that Tsongkhapa's view is out of step with today's society and so we have to go back to what Gautama Buddha meant by sexual misconduct. He wanted us to reflect on our acts and see if they bring harm or are helpful. So in this context, I believe if we want to know if an act constitutes sexual misconduct or not, we should ask ourselves the following questions:

Does the act cause harm or does it bring joy?
Is the act motivated by love and understanding?
Would you like it if someone did it to you?
Is there mutual consent?

If there is mutual consent between two adults, it is not abusive and is an expression of love, respect and loyalty, I believe it cannot be classified as sexual misconduct, irrespective of whether it is between a man and a woman, two men or two women.

As I stated earlier, I do not believe religions should get involved with people's sexuality. We cannot choose our sexual orientation, as we cannot choose our race or gender, so it is cruel to penalise someone for something out of their control. So in answer to the two questions posed at the beginning of this piece, I believe homosexuality should not be forbidden in Buddhism, and homosexuals should not be made to feel guilty for loving someone of the same sex. I also believe homosexuality should not be regarded as sexual misconduct if it is not causing harm, and is loving and consensual.

29

Buddhist Views on Euthanasia

Euthanasia, taken from a Greek word meaning a good death, refers to the practice of intentionally ending a life to relieve pain and suffering. There are two different types of euthanasia, namely, voluntary and involuntary. Voluntary euthanasia is when death is hastened with the consent of the dying person, and involuntary is when no consent is possible because the dying person is brain dead or in a long term coma.

It can be further divided into active and passive euthanasia. Active is when something is done to end life, such as a lethal injection, and passive is when treatment is withdrawn and nature is left to take its course. Laws on euthanasia are different from country to country, so here I am only looking at the moral implications of euthanasia and not the legal.

Buddhism places great emphasis on not killing living beings, in fact, it is the first of the five precepts. So at first glance you would think euthanasia is wrong within Buddhism. However, it has to be noted that the precepts are not hard and fast rules, and were given as training rules and not commandments. Also, in Buddhism great emphasis is given to Compassion. So if someone is dying in terrible agony, wouldn't it be an act of compassion to hasten their death, with their consent or after consulting a doctor?

As with all contentious issues, there are countless different viewpoints. Here I have selected three that I feel give a good cross section of opinions from within the Buddhist community. Firstly, Dalai Lama stated that all life is precious and so it is better to avoid euthanasia. However, he further stated that there are exceptional cases and so each case should be judged on an individual basis. This seems to leave room for euthanasia in certain circumstances.

Secondly, Thanssaro Bhikkhu, a Buddhist monk and scholar, stated that Gautama Buddha did not try and ease the patient's transition to death, but concentrated on insight into suffering and its end. So, he believes that from Gautama Buddha's perspective, encouraging a sick person to relax their grip on life or to give up the will to live would not count as an act of compassion. It seems the bhikkhu believes it is more compassionate to watch a loved one die in agony.

Thirdly, Lama Zopa Rinpoche stated he was more concerned with the outcome of the person's next life. He said that people think performing euthanasia is an act of compassion, but he believed it also has to be carried out with wisdom. If the person will have more peace and happiness in their next life, the act will be good, however it may mean the person is reborn in a lower realm and their suffering will be a million times worse.

He went on to say that if a person is going to stay in a coma for many years, rather than spending thousands of dollars keeping them alive, support should be withdrawn and the money used to purify their negative karma, which may cause them to suffer in future lives. This approach is fine if there is a next life, but I cannot honestly be sure of that fact, can you?

So in Buddhism it seems to boil down to these three factors; the precept of not killing, compassion and wisdom.

Gautama Buddha taught the precepts so we do not cause harm to ourselves and others. If we turn them into rules we run the risk of them becoming detached from human suffering. This in turn will lead us down the wrong path and could cause us to harm others in the name of Buddhism. Compassion should be educated and informed. It should stem from our own experiences and understanding of the world. It should not be an act of sympathy, but should be empathic. If it is carried out in this way, it is coming from wisdom.

My own personal view is that euthanasia should be viewed on a case by case basis. It has to be a three way decision, if possible, between the patient, the family and the medical team. If the patient is not able to be involved, then the other two parties have to do what they believe is correct and kind. Of course life is precious, but if someone has totally lost their quality of life and will never recover from their illness, it seems euthanasia is the kindest approach.

If your loved one was lying in excruciating pain with a terminal illness, what do you think is the compassionate and wise thing to do? Should you let them suffer in this life, hoping that their next life will be better, or should you relieve them of their agony in the here and now? These are not easy questions to answer and I pray that I never have to, but if I do, I hope I would act out of compassion and not hide behind ancient texts or what someone thought Gautama Buddha said or didn't say.

If you find yourself in this awful situation at the moment, my heart goes out to you and I hope you are able to find some inner strength.

As this is such a personal issue, I believe we should talk about it to our relatives and loved ones. This way they will know your opinion should anything like this ever happen to you.

30

What are the Fruits of being Generous?

At certain times of the year our thoughts turn towards giving and so I thought I would write something about the art of giving. What I am talking about here is generosity. This played a big part in Gautama Buddha's teachings, as it was mentioned on numerous occasions. In the Itivuttaka, a collection of 112 short discourses, he told us about the fruit of giving:

> 'If beings knew, as I know, the fruit of sharing gifts, they would not enjoy their use without sharing them, nor would the taint of stinginess obsess the heart and stay there. Even if it were their last bite, their last morsel of food, they would not enjoy its use without sharing it, if there were anyone to receive it.'

So what are the fruits of being generous? I believe, for the giver, they help foster a clear conscience; help you build a good future; make you compassionate and a respected person within society. It also gives you a great feeling inside. A feeling of warmth, pleasure and satisfaction. Many people think we shouldn't receive anything in return for giving, but this is not being totally honest. If we give a gift to a child and they smile warmly at you, you are going to feel happy inside. If you take a sick person to hospital, they are going to be grateful and you will feel that you have done a good deed. So it is of course true we receive something from giving.

However, having said that, we shouldn't give just to receive these things. They should just be looked upon as a by-product and not the purpose for giving. In the Anguttara Nikaya it states five types of rewards of giving:

> 'These are the five rewards of generosity: One is dear and appealing to people in society, one is admired by good people, one's good name is spread about, one does not stray from the rightful duties of the householder and at the time of death, one reappears in a good destination.'

One of the key things generosity does is stop us becoming miserly. It gives us temporary relief from the pain of selfishness and stops us getting totally wrapped up in ourselves. When we are miserly we worry day and night about our wealth and belongings. We go to great lengths to protect them. We can't sleep at night worrying if someone will break in and steal them. We grow to mistrust others and our mind is disturbed by all of the pressure of protecting our wealth. It seems the miser is so scared of losing his wealth he hordes it. In the Samyutta Nikaya, Gautama Buddha said:

> 'What the miser fears, that keeps him from giving, is the very danger that comes when he doesn't give.'

How true is that? So a miser lives in fear of his wealth, but for what benefit? When we die we are not able to take anything with us, so isn't it nicer to give them away while we are alive? I am not talking about giving everything away and living a life as a pauper. But there is only so much wealth and belongings we need or can use in this life.

If we do give, we have to be careful that our generosity stems from compassion and not from pride. Our intention and motivation is extremely important here. If you are giving just to get thanks or praise it isn't going to benefit you in the ways I mentioned above. Your conscience is not going to be clear; you will not become more compassionate, reduce your suffering and you certainly will not get respect from others. Giving something and expecting praise is not a very attractive trait.

How does generosity help clear our conscience and reduce our suffering? Well, Gautama Buddha's teachings are mainly concerned with our state of mind and generosity is about having non-attachment to or craving for things. He stated in the four truths that our suffering stems from our craving and attachment to things, so without this craving and attachment our minds become clearer, happier and a little freer, which in turn means less suffering. In the Dana Sutra it states three mental factors of giving:

'The donor, before giving, is glad; while giving, his/her mind is inspired; and after giving, is gratified.'

There are three different types of giving that Gautama Buddha mentioned. The first covers giving something away we no longer want. This doesn't ask too much of us, as we have already finished with the thing we are giving away. I am thinking of old clothes and books. It is a kind of recycling.

The second is giving away something that we would like to receive ourselves, such as new clothes, the latest mobile, book or CD. There is a lot of thoughtfulness and caring in this type of giving.

The third, and final, type is giving away something that is very dear to us, such as a painting we cherish or some personal jewellery. These types of giving shows that we are not attached and understand impermanence. Though it is the most difficult for us to engage in.

Giving doesn't just mean material things. It could be a friendly smile or kind, encouraging words. But whatever you are giving you have to ensure it doesn't conflict with the precepts or any other code of ethics.

Whatever type of giving you do, do it with an open heart. Do not expect praise and thanks. Let the smile on the person's face be all the thanks you need.

31

Why Meditate?

This is an age old question and one I am asked a lot. So why should we make time to meditate? Hopefully, I will be able to give you some answers to this question in this article. I am not going to fill it with scientific proof that you can find for yourselves on the internet. What I want to mention is my own experience of meditation and how it has helped me. Now, I must say at the outset that just because I experience meditation in a certain way, it doesn't mean you will have the exact same experience. We are all different and you should keep this in mind whilst reading this post.

So, what are the benefits of meditating? I have listed below some of the benefits I have experienced over the last 20 years or so.

1. Firstly, meditation can help us to understand our inner self. We all carry around concepts and beliefs we have learnt from parents, school, friends, society, religions and so on. Sometimes these concepts are outdated and are no longer serving us in a helpful way. However,

because we have been acting in such a way for many years, these concepts have become a habit. So meditation helps us to look at what is driving us, what makes us act in a certain way. We can only make changes to our way of thinking once we are fully in-tune with our inner self. It is at that point we are able to let go of our harmful concepts and only engage with our helpful ones.

2. Meditation helps calm down our restless mind. Every year we go on holiday to give ourselves a break, but what about giving our minds a break? This is where meditation comes in. It gives us mental relief. If our mind is stressed and under a lot of pressure, we will not be able to make the right decisions. But if it is calm and relaxed, we will be more able to make a good decision. Also, a clear mind helps you concentrate better and so will improve your productivity. In meditation we are giving ourselves a period of freedom from our daily chores and the things that are stressing us out.

3. Meditation is good for our health. If we are frustrated, impatient, suffering from stress and tension, becoming angry very easily, we are obviously going to harm ourselves internally, which in turn will damage our quality of life. By meditating we are helping to alleviate these things and become more patient, tolerant and stress-free. This in turn helps to reduce our blood pressure and, it is claimed, can also strengthen our immune systems (this is because one cause of a weak

immune system is stress, so meditation will help reduce your stress and strengthen your immune system).

What these three points show clearly is that meditation helps improve your quality of life. It helps you to find what is driving you and what outdated concepts and beliefs are causing you to suffer. It helps you to calm your mind and free yourself from stress. It is also good for your mental health and the quality of your mind. I believe these three points go some way to answering the question, why meditate?

If you are still not sure if working on your mind is important, give this some thought:

Whatever you achieve in your life is the result of your actions.

The actions you choose to take are the result of the decisions you make.

The decisions you make stem from your thinking processes. These thinking processes are completely dependent on the quality of your mind.

I hope you can now see why you should give meditation a go. Some people are not willing to try it out until they have firm scientific evidence, for you guys, I would suggest you have a look on the internet at the scientific evidence. Others are happy just to give it a go on the back of someone else's experience. So for you I hope this post has encouraged you to sit on a cushion and give it a go.

32

Inner Questioning

It's not the answers you get from others, but the questions you ask yourself that will help you reduce your suffering. Give this statement some thought. Is it true? I believe so.

The answers from other people come from their take on the world, which is coloured by their concepts, perceptions, experiences and world view. It may be completely different from your experiences, concepts and so on. This is why I believe other people's answers are less important than your own inner questioning.

For me the most important question I keep asking myself is, 'What am I holding on to that I should be letting go of? Before we can properly answer this question, we need to firstly understand that everything changes, and that includes your relationships, lifestyle, hopes, dreams, thoughts, feelings and emotions.

So change is not only possible, it is a fact of life, but how many times have you heard people say that they have always been an angry (insert whatever negative emotion you want here) person? Instead of trying to change, they simply carry on the way things are. OK, I get it; it is easier to just carry on instead of making changes, because it feels safe, it is your comfort zone. But remember, just because something seemed to work in the past, doesn't mean it is going to work in the present moment. Everything from your past does not belong in your present.

Now this type of self questioning can be painful, because we have to be totally honest with ourselves. We have to take a critical look at our inner most workings. We have to see ourselves, warts and all. Believe me it isn't easy, but the rewards can be enormous.

In my experience the best time to look at what is working in your life and what isn't, is the end of each day. Sit quietly in the evening and look back over the day. See what situations worked for you and what didn't. Remember the things that worked and make a mental note to act in that way again.

Now look at situations that didn't work out quite the way you would have hoped. Look deeply into why they didn't work out. Was it because of jealousy, pride, anger, desire, aversion or some other destructive emotion, thought or feeling? Remember, these thoughts, feelings and emotions stem from your mind, so don't go blaming others. That is not going to help you.

Once you understand the root of the problem, you can start to mentally work through a more positive scenario. See in your mind's eye what it would have been like if you weren't driven by destructive thoughts, feelings and emotions. See what a more positive outcome looks like. This will help you act in a different way next time this situation arises.

This practice takes time, so don't expect instant results, because you are going to be disappointed. However, I strongly believe that the relationship you have with yourself is the closest and most important relationship you will ever have.

One final point, you don't have control over every little thing that happens to you, but you do have control over the way you react to it.

33

Just Sitting and Letting Our Thoughts Be

I wrote the following in February, 2013, 'Truth is found in silence and stillness. It is not found in activity. Doing ritual practice, reciting mantra, studying Buddhist philosophy and participating in voluntary work are all good things to do, and are very helpful in putting you on the right path. But they are activities and so your mind is agitated. Truth will only come when you sit down and meditate or reflect. When your mind is calm, still and silent.'

I was recently sitting on a bench, in a busy shopping centre, people watching, and these words came back to me. I was observing people frantically rushing from pillar to post. I started to wonder if they ever just sat in stillness and silence, or did they spend their lives on full speed ahead. When was the last time you just sat in silence, not planning the future or worrying about the past? Can you even remember?

We rush around, filling every waking hour, trying to get some peace and happiness in our lives, but the irony is, these cannot be found in activity. We may be able to find fleeting moments of happiness, but they are soon gone and we are back to having that uneasy feeling in our mind. Calmness can only be found in stillness and silence. Not the silence you get from turning off your iPhone, but the silence of just sitting and letting your thoughts be.

How much happier life would be if we just spent ten to fifteen minutes a day just watching our thoughts arise, and then just letting them be. Not engaging with them, just observing them. Not judging them, just watching them come and go. Not being engrossed with what has happened or what we want to happen, but just engulfing ourselves in the stillness of the moment. Oh how our lives would be so much calmer and more peaceful.

I know this sounds very simplistic, but actually this is what can happen when we give ourselves the time to just be. Don't take my word for it, try it for yourself. Commit to sitting in silence, just observing your thoughts coming and going, for ten minutes a day for 21 days, and I assure you, you will feel the difference.

Our lives are complicated enough, so shouldn't we take the time to just sit in stillness and release some of our tension? It seems like a no-brainer to me.

34

Teachers – for Learning or Leaning

I strongly believe that if we want to follow Gautama Buddha's teachings we need to find ourselves a good teacher. Someone who not only has experience of what he or she is teaching, but also does the practice. In other words, they should practice what they preach.

But what do we need the teacher for? I think we need them to guide, mentor and support us along our chosen path. They should pass on their knowledge and understanding, and be there for us when we run into obstacles. Gautama Buddha placed great emphasis on personal experience, so I see the teacher's role as a 'helping hand' along the way, and someone who helps us make sense of our own experiences and not tell us what we should be experiencing.

The key to a good teacher/student relationship is that we learn from them, but not get attached to them. A lot of teachers want exclusive rights over their students, but I personally think it is fine to have more than one teacher at a time, and it is also fine to move on once we have learnt what we can from them – we can always go back and get advice if we hit an obstacle.

If we see the teacher as a guide, mentor or spiritual friend, we are not going to get into problems of attachment or let ourselves be abused by them. However, if we see the teacher as a higher being, a precious one or some kind of guru figure, we are leaving ourselves open to all sorts of manipulation. When we see the teacher in that way we are not there to learn from them, but to lean on them. We are using them as a mental crutch and abdicating our responsibilities. Wisdom and compassion, the two wings of Buddhism, cannot be found in this way.

Some people think their teacher has all the answers, they can see and hear everything and they have special powers whereby they can magically tell the future, walk through walls or fly in the air. I believe these are all projections and not based on any kind of reality.

If you see your teacher in that way you should ask yourself these questions, 'What do I need a teacher for?' 'Is it to learn from them or lean on them?' 'Am I looking for a way to reduce my suffering or just some sort of magical trip?'

The most important aspect of Buddhism, I believe, is that it is an inner journey. A journey of discovery about what makes us who we are, why we act in a certain way and how we can reduce the suffering in our life. For me it is not about mythical figures or realms, I see those as the outside world. It is about trying to make myself the best possible person I can in this life and that is why I need a teacher, or teachers, to help me explore my inner world. I don't want to lean on them, I have my friends for that, I want to learn from them.

What do you need a teacher for? Are you a learner or a leaner?

35

The virtue of patience

As the saying goes, 'patience is a virtue,' and it certainly is. It can also be an antidote to anger and hatred. However, it is sometimes quite difficult to be patient. When I was in my twenties it was the one thing I had very little of. I had just been promoted to manager and I had very few man-management skills, so I wanted things done as soon as I mentioned them, not only that, I wanted them done my way, because I was manager and I knew best – really, I actually used to think like that. I cringe now thinking about it. I used to think that people really tried my patience, until I started to follow Gautama Buddha's teachings and then I realised the problem was actually mine. There was nothing outside of me causing my impatience, it all stemmed from my own mind. The problem wasn't what people were doing; it was the way I was reacting to what they were doing.

I had one teaching where the teacher explained a jug is filled drop by drop. That really struck a chord with me, because it made me realise things are achieved slowly, and whenever I started to get impatient I would recall those words, and that helped me to calm down.

Although patience in itself is a virtue, it also shows that you have other virtues as well, such as forgiveness, tolerance and forbearance. It further shows that you have concern for other people and their views, you have compassion towards others and you have an open mind. So a lot is attached to this simple word. In the Kakacupama Sutra, Gautama Buddha gave this advice:

> '...if anyone were to reproach you right to your face, even then you should abandon those urges and thoughts which are worldly. There you should train yourself thus: 'Neither shall my mind be affected by this, nor shall I give vent to evil words; but I shall remain full of concern and pity, with a mind of love, and I shall not give in to hatred.' This is how you should train yourself.'

So what is patience? It is unconditionally accepting what is happening right now in the present moment. When you lack patience you are rejecting the present moment, substituting some future moment from your imagination, thinking that this future moment will help solve the imagined problem with the present moment. So we can only have patience when we are present in the moment.

Patience and the lack of it are emotions and can be worked on during your meditation session. When I looked back over my day and saw that I had been impatient, which in the early years was quite a lot, I would see that the only person who was suffering greatly was me. I was making myself agitated, tense and angry. It was only after looking closely at my impatience that I could start to let it be. Now, I cannot say my impatience has gone forever, that would be unreasonable, but I am able to catch it as it rises and then let it be.

Some people believe that by meditating we will be able to stop all of our emotions and feelings from arising, which seems to be a common misunderstanding in Buddhism. I think it is impossible to stop our emotions and feelings from arising, but we can at least be aware of them when they do arise. This way we will be able to let them be and not just blindly follow them. I am going to digress a little bit here, but I just want to tell you a story about stopping your emotions.

I read a book once written by a Western lama (someone who has done a three year retreat) and he was recounting the day of 9/11. He said that he was so far into his practice that he had no emotions when watching the plane fly into the tower. He didn't feel that it was good or bad. He said he didn't feel anything. I am not sure I believe him. If we were able to fully stop our emotions, we would just become a cabbage. If I thought Gautama Buddha's teachings were going to do that to me, I would stop practicing straight away. If a teacher promises you that his practice can stop your emotions, run as fast as you can. What we are looking for is an understanding of what triggers them and have an antidote ready for when they arrive. We have to face up to them and not try to transcend them. Emotions help us see right from wrong, pleasure from pain, so by removing them we are removing a built in value system. This value system has built up over the years from our experiences, and even though these experiences are filtered through our view of the world, they are still a valuable tool for us to distinguish what is socially acceptable.

If you are an impatient person you have to work out why that is. It is usually because you are trying to multi-task, you have set yourself an impossibly tight schedule or you think you know better than others. You may just be feeling anxious, unhappy or worried and not even know that it is because of impatience. It really does help to be aware and your mindfulness and meditation session is a great tool for that. You can look for patterns and triggers, and then work on an antidote.

36

An Open-Mind Starts with Humility

I always feel that a humble person is easy to be around. They do not waste time on bragging about what they have, who they are or where they have been. They play down their achievements and are more attentive to other's needs.

Whereas, the opposite of this is someone who is proud and conceited. Both things are not attractive traits. It really is difficult, for me, to spend a lot of time with someone who is boasting. They are only interested in selling themselves and have no interest in who you are or what you think or know.

I have always found people with pride to also have the biggest egos – and usually, the biggest mouths to go with it. But a humble person is quiet, respectful and attentive. Which one would you rather be around? Or for that matter, which one would you rather be?

Another trait of a proud and conceited person is that they are not open minded and they are not willing to learn from others, as they think they already know everything. Now this is something we have to guard against as we move along our chosen path. If we start to think we are making great progress and we are already better than the people around us, we are going to run up against obstacles, such as pride.

We have to stay open minded. Just because we know a way to do something, it doesn't mean another person doesn't know a better or easier way. We shouldn't assume we know best. A humble person will continue to learn throughout their live.

Once we become a proud and egotistical person, it is very hard to subdue these emotions. So it is better not to travel down that road in the first place.

We have to also be mindful of people praising us. They maybe flattering you because of your position or they want something. However, it maybe that you are worthy of praise, but be careful, our ego loves to be praised and it may lead to pride if we are not mindful.

So what are the causes of pride? There are many, but two main causes are; dualistic thinking and an inflated sense of self.

When people think in a dualistic way it can stir up pride, because they start thinking I am good and others are bad; I'm handsome, they are ugly; I'm intelligent and they are stupid. It is this type of thinking that causes us to fixate on 'I am this,' 'I am that.' We start to emphasis the sense of self, which leads us to get attached to who we think we are. Both of these lead to pride and conceit. In the Nipata Sutra Gautama Buddha stated this:

> 'By being alert and attentive, he begins to let go of cravings as they arise. But whatever he begins to accomplish, he should be aware of inner pride. He must avoid thinking of himself as better than another or worse or equal, for that is all comparison and emphasises the self'.

In 'The Thirty-Seven Practices of a Bodhisattva' it advises us how we should act, even if we are rich or famous:

Even when you are famous, honoured by all
And as rich as the god of wealth himself,
 Know that success in the world is ephemeral
And don't let it go to your head – this is the practice of a
bodhisattva.
(Translation by Ken McLeod in his book 'Reflections on
Silver River'. A bodhisattva, as explained in this excellent
book, is a person who lives and breathes compassion)

So it is clear that humility is a trait we have to work at, or we could find ourselves getting wrapped up in pride. The pride I am talking about here is our over inflated sense of self. It is not the pride we have for our children, loved ones and so on. This pride stems from love and compassion, whereas, our over inflated sense of self type of pride stems from our ego.

37

The Importance of a Balanced Life Style

It is very important for us to have a balanced lifestyle. This means we have to live within our means. In the Vyagghapajja Sutra, Gautama Buddha stated this:

"....... a householder knowing his income and expenses leads a balanced life, neither extravagant nor miserly, knowing that thus his income will stand in excess of his expenses, but not his expenses in excess of his income. Just as the goldsmith, or an apprentice of his, knows, on holding up a balance, that by so much it has dipped down, by so much it has tilted up; even so a householder, knowing his income and expenses leads a balanced life, neither extravagant nor miserly, knowing that thus his income will stand in excess of his expenses, but not his expenses in excess of his income."

As we all know, the world is going through an especially difficult time financially at the moment. This is, in part, due to people's greed. People have been seduced by material things,

things they cannot afford, and so they have bought them on credit. They have been given mortgages they can never repay. They are living a life on borrowed money. Gautama Buddha's words above seem very relevant at the moment.

We are bombarded everyday with advertisements telling us we need this or that to make our lives complete. It seems our culture implicitly values desires, and we evaluate the worth of people by what they own. Corporations, hungry for profit, tell us that ladies need this cream to look young, men need to use this razor to look handsome, children need these toys to be happy, and families need to drive around in a big gas-guzzling SUV— we are constantly barraged by new products. There appears to be a new smart phone, TV or electronic gadget released every week. Greed seems to be considered a virtue and not something to avoid.

A balanced life is one whereby we ensure that our income exceeds our expenditures. This is not an easy task to undertake as we look around and see that everyone has the latest iPhone or iPad, and that includes our peers, friends and family. The pressure is on us to conform, but we have to resist this pressure. It isn't easy and takes a lot of discipline, but it is doable.

The trick is not to be led along by our desires. We have to look at the things we need to get by and the things that are just a luxury. Buddhism would not say you shouldn't have luxuries, but it would say that we need to prevent ourselves from getting attached to them. There is no suffering in products, but there is suffering in our attachment to these products.

Obviously, we need food, clothes and a roof over our heads—these are our basic needs—but we must think carefully about other things that set off our desires. If you need the latest smart phone and have the money to cover it, then go ahead.

However, if you cannot cover the cost and need to pay for it on credit, I would say leave it until you have saved enough money. I always feel happier when I have saved for something; the product then seems to mean more to me.

So check your desires, and don't let peer pressure or multibillion-dollar companies make you overspend. Live a balanced life because you will feel a lot happier and less stressed by acting in this way—no matter what the advertisers tell you.

38

A Drop of Mindfulness

I think it's true to say, we spend most of our waking hours fixating on the past or the future. We relive painful experiences from our past, or construct elaborate scenarios of what we think may happen in the future – but, in my experience, very rarely does. This brings us untold mental suffering. We never stop to check our thoughts, feelings or emotions. We just blindly follow them. This makes us act in an unskilful way. I believe a big part of what we think is, quite frankly, total rubbish. We do not need to blindly follow every thought, but sadly we do. What we are doing is torturing ourselves, but happily, there is another way.

When we stop trudging back to the past or flitting off to the future, we become present in the moment. We start to become aware of our thoughts, feelings, emotions and body sensations. It is a truly liberating experience. This is what people popularly call mindfulness.

Mindfulness is when we are paying attention to what is happening in the present moment. We become aware of what thoughts are arising, what we are feeling, what emotions are present and what sensations we feel in the body. We get a full moment-by-moment experience. This helps calm and steady the mind, so we are able to see which thoughts we should follow, and which we should drop, like a hot potato.

When we are being mindful we are looking at our mind in a non-judgemental way. We are just observing with equanimity, and not trying to control or suppress our thoughts. All we have to do is remain present with our thoughts, feelings and emotions, whether they happen to be pleasant or unpleasant. This gives us the chance to reflect before we act. It allows us to look at what is arising in an open, friendly and more compassionate way. It gives us a choice - act or don't act. If what is arising is helpful, we should act upon it. However, if it is unskilful and harmful, we should not act and just let the thought go.

When our mind is agitated it is like a bucket of muddy water. However, when we are being present in the moment, the mud settles and we can see clearly. We are able to see just what is present, be it anger, pride, fear, jealousy, excitement and so on. This insight gives us choices. We no longer need to follow whatever comes into our minds. We can decide on the most skilful way to act. This will help reduce our suffering and the suffering of those around us.

You may think this sounds wonderful, but impossible to do. Well it's not. Do this little experiment – sit quietly with your eyes slightly closed. Now become aware of the sensation as your breath enters and leaves your nostril. Do this five times. Congratulations, you have just been mindful. You weren't thinking about the past or the future, but just present in the moment. Of course, mindfulness takes practice, but like everything else, the more we do it the easier it becomes.

Start off slowly and incorporate more acts from your daily routine as you become more experienced. Try cleaning your teeth in a mindful way. Become fully aware of the task you are doing and don't allow your thoughts to go off to the past or the future. Experience what you feel when you hold your toothbrush and squeeze the toothpaste. Focus on the sensation of the toothbrush going up and down in your mouth. Taste the toothpaste on your teeth. Feel your arm moving up and down. Experience the sensations in your mouth once you have finished cleaning your teeth. These are all moments of mindfulness. You are going to feel like this is the first time you have ever cleaned your teeth, and in a way, it is. It is the first time you have cleaned them mindfully.

39

Are You a Donkey pretending to be a Cow?

Let me ask you a question, 'what is the most favourable time to receive teachings?' I believe it is when we are able to fully connect with the teaching. I don't know about you, but I have sat through teachings and not really taken very much of them on board. I am physically there, but mentally I am off in my own world. So this undoubtedly isn't a favourable time.

Some people go to as many teachings as possible, thinking this is what being a Buddhist is all about. They believe that even if they don't listen or try to understand the teaching, it will leave an imprint on their mind for their next life. I know when I first moved to India, I spent a great part of my first few years at one teaching or another. I wasn't fully taking them in, and I certainly didn't give myself time to implement them. Buddhism was just an identity for me. So again, this was not a favourable time for me to receive any teachings.

We are humans, and we all like to belong to some group or club, whether it is a football team, religion, yoga club or gym—we all identify with something. However, Buddhism isn't really about identity; it is about changing oneself by implementing the teachings. Gautama Buddha gave some advice on this subject in an amusing discourse called Gadrabha Sutra:

'It is just as if a donkey were following right after a herd of cattle, saying, "I too am a cow! I too am a cow!" Its colour is not that of a cow, its voice is not that of a cow, its hoof is not that of a cow, and yet it still keeps following right after the herd of cattle, saying, "I too am a cow! I too am a cow!"

'In the same way, there is the case where a certain person follows right after a community of Buddhists, saying, "I too am a Buddhist! I too am a Buddhist!" He doesn't have the other Buddhists' desire for undertaking the training in heightened virtue, doesn't have their desire for undertaking the training in heightened mind [concentration], doesn't have their desire for undertaking the training in heightened discernment, and yet he still keeps following right after the community of Buddhists, saying, "I too am a Buddhist! I too am a Buddhist!"

'So you should train yourselves: "Strong will be our desire for undertaking the training in heightened virtue; strong will be our desire for undertaking the training in heightened mind [concentration]; strong will be our desire for undertaking the training in heightened discernment." That is how you should train yourselves'.

So it isn't about an identity, accumulating teachings or just understanding them intellectually. It is about being motivated to change your present condition. But before we can do that, we need to know that our present condition isn't working or that we are suffering. We all know when we have physical suffering, but mental suffering is a bit harder to pin down. Gautama

Buddha stated that there are three types of suffering, and I will briefly go through them here.

First, there is the suffering of pain. This is when we have a cold, headache, cancer or Ebola, or we are sad, lonely and so on. This is easy for us to understand. This type of suffering is described as painful when it arises, painful when it remains and pleasurable when it changes.

The second one is the suffering of happiness and is a little harder to understand. Our happiness is based on causes and conditions, and so it is compounded, and anything compounded is, by its very nature, impermanent. So this happiness is not going to last, and when it ends, our suffering starts. This type of suffering is pleasurable when it arises and remains, but painful when it changes.

The final suffering is the all-pervasive suffering. This is the most difficult to understand. This type of suffering is within everything in our lives, but because it is suffering on a subtle level, we are prone to miss it. It is a condition that exists because of how we perceive ourselves in relation to the world. Our entire worldly experience is a definition of suffering that we cannot even see. We see ourselves and the world as separate— I'm here and the world is outside of me—in other words, as subject and object. We see ourselves as a solid, independent self. But Gautama Buddha taught that this is not actually the case and we are all interconnected. So the way we look at things— subject and object, me and everything else—is in some way the cause of our suffering that will come back to us in the future. This type of suffering is described as not being apparent when it arises, remains or ceases, but it is still a cause of our suffering.

Many people keep suffering because it doesn't occur to them that there may be a better way to live their lives. So once we know that we are suffering and there is another way to be, we can make a decision to try and change. That will motivate us to listen to the teachings more intently. The teachings should give you an insight into how you can change for the better. But to do this we must have confidence in the teachings and the teacher, or we are not going to be overly receptive. I am not talking about blind faith, but just a feeling that what is being said may be of help to you. Of course, once you have implemented the teachings and found, from your own experience, that they work, your trust will be based on something more solid. But at first we have to have the courage to embrace the teachings and this will make them favourable.

Don't think that every time you receive a teaching it is going to be at a favourable time. You may have to have the same teaching several times before the penny drops. I have sat through many teachings again and again, but every now and then the teacher says something that I have heard many times, but this time a light comes on in my head—I finally got the point.

So we need perseverance. If we really want a change within ourselves it is not going to come easily; it takes work. Perseverance is a skill that seems to be in short supply these days. We are so used to having things handed to us on a plate and all our communications reduced to sound bites that we seem to lack any sense of perseverance.

So to create this favourable time we have to know we are suffering, have trust in the teachings and then be motivated, confident, patient and, above all, have perseverance. We then have to give ourselves space where we can fully engage with the teachings. We need to contemplate what we have heard, how it fits in with our experience of life and how we can implement it as a tool for change.

Sometimes we will go to teachings because we know the teacher will validate what we already believe. This type of teaching is not overly helpful or favourable. It is harder, and so more beneficial, to go to a teaching where you hear things that challenge your beliefs. This is because it makes you investigate what is driving you. It gives you a chance to look deeply into what your beliefs are based on. This is far more favourable than simple validation.

To finish, here are five rewards we can obtain by listening intently to the teachings. These come from the Dhammassavana Sutra:

'There are these five rewards in listening to the teachings. Which five? One hears what one has not heard before. One clarifies what one has heard before. One gets rid of doubt. One's views are made straight. One's mind grows calm and stable. These are the five rewards in listening to the teachings'.

40

We just go Through Life Taking it for Granted

I live in Northern India and we recently had two days of very cold, driving rain. One of my students, Arun, looked out of his window and saw a young man sitting under a tree. He was soaking wet and shivering. Arun tried to encourage him to take shelter, but due to the guys mental health issues he didn't respond. Arun took him food, a hot drink and a plastic sheet. The next morning Arun again looked out of his window and the young man was still sitting exactly where he had left him the night before. Compassion arose in Arun and he finally understood just how precious his life is.

Sometimes it takes an incident like this to make us realise just how fortunate we really are. We just go through life taking it for granted. In fact, we even take breathing for granted. Breathing in and out, day after day, year after year, we forget how amazing that truly is. Just think if we had to pay for the air we breathe, I am sure we wouldn't be able to afford it. We might think we do not have much in our life, but when we consider it, to be able to breathe is a great fortune.

Even when we have things we are never satisfied. We have clothes to wear, but that isn't enough for us, we want the best clothes. We have food to eat, but again that isn't enough, we want the most delicious food. We are never satisfied. We never count our blessings.

Our life span is short; it is like dewdrops on the tip of a blade of grass. If you think about it, there are very few causes of life, but an enormous amount of causes of death. So we should not be over confident that we are going to be alive tomorrow.

Some may think this is depressing and not very helpful, but I beg to differ. If we understand how precious our life is we will become contented, compassionate and, dare I say it, happier.

Your life is precious, so please spare a thought for those who are not as fortunate as you.

I will let Dalai Lama have the last say on this subject:

Today I am fortunate to have woken up,
I am alive, I have a precious human life,
I am not going to waste it,
I am going to use all my energies to develop myself.
To expand my heart out to others,
To become awakened for the benefit of all beings,
I am going to have kind thoughts towards others,
I am not going to get angry, or think badly about others.
I am going to benefit others as much as I can."

41

Being Human

Imagine no possessions
I wonder if you can
No need for greed or hunger
A brotherhood of man
Imagine all the people
Sharing all the world...
You may say I'm a dreamer
But I'm not the only one
I hope someday you'll join us
And the world will live as one

A brotherhood of man seems such a dream at the moment, and as for sharing the world, forget it. We are so far removed from a world where we can live as one, in fact, we have very little tolerance for the views of others and seem hell-bent on pursuing our own selfish ideology.

We identify with religions, political parties, football teams, countries and so on, but we never identify with the one thing that binds us together – being humans.

At the core of all religions is compassion for our fellow man, but this has been lost among so much dogma. In the 21st century religions are still being run by men. Not just any men, but rich and powerful men. Men who are afraid of change.

In Christianity you are told to love thy neighbour, but not if he is gay. Muslims are being told to love only other Muslims, and now Buddhists are starting to follow suit. In Myanmar, Sri Lanka and Thailand, Buddhists have grown intolerant of Muslims and are burning their houses and even killing them. This is from a religion based on non-violence.

However, the religions are not to blame. It is the fanatical people using religions for their own personal ideology that are causing all the problems. These fanatics are within all religions and they are slowly turning the world into a dangerous place. These people are filled with only hatred and ignorance.

Where will it all end? Nobody knows the answer to this, but sooner or later people have to stand up and say enough is enough. We cannot survive in a world driven by killing, fear and discrimination. By sitting on the fence and becoming immune to the violence around us, we moderate people are going to become part of the problem. The moderate people within the various religions, and these are thankfully the majority, have to speak out sooner rather than later. Tolerance is the only answer.

I envisage a world where we all have tolerance for others. A world where we accept difference and not fear it. You may say I'm a dreamer, but I hope and pray I am not the only one.

42

A Big Pot of Merit

Merit is a concept commonly found in Hinduism and Buddhism. In a lot of Buddhist circles people believe if they do good in this life it will mean a good rebirth. This is how they see merit, it is something to accumulate. However, this implies that you score points by doing good deeds, and this goes into some imaginary pot and is miraculously taken into your next life. This seems to be quite a naive view point.

I believe this is not how merit should be viewed. I think if we do a good deed it will leave a positive impression or imprint on our mind. The by-product of that is happiness – something we are all striving for. We feel good when we help others and it makes us a more kind, caring and compassionate person – not in the next life, but in this life.

Gautama Buddha stated ten meritorious ways we can act:

1. Giving Alms – this doesn't mean just giving to monks or monasteries, but to all people less fortunate than ourselves.

2. Observing Virtue – this in its basic form means trying to adhere to the five precepts, which are refraining from

killing, stealing, lying, sexually inappropriate acts and intoxicants.

3. Developing Concentration – here we are talking about meditation and mindfulness. The only way we can really get to understand ourselves is through mindfulness, and obtain an understanding of Gautama Buddha's teachings is through meditation. If we understand ourselves and the teachings we will guard our minds from negative thoughts, which in turn mean our actions will be helpful and not harmful.

4. Honouring others – we can do this through polite, kind and modest conduct. If someone has been kind to you, such as a parent, teacher, friend, acquaintance or stranger, you should return that kindness.

5. Offering Service – lots of people study, meditate and teach about compassion, but very few actually put it into practice. We have to get off of our meditation cushions and get out into the community to help others.

6. Dedicating Your Merit to Others – this act stops us having too much pride and becoming too conceited. Maybe we are good people and help others, so instead of feeling that we are special people, we offer our meritorious imprints to others. It has to be remembered that this is a mental act, and we are not actually taking our merit and putting it into someone else's pot.

7. Rejoicing in Other's Merit – instead of us becoming jealous or having thoughts of ill-will when someone else

has gained merit, we actually rejoice and give them encouragement.

8. Understanding Gautama Buddha's Teachings – we should listen, understand, ask questions to clear up any doubts, meditate and implement Gautama Buddha's teachings. This way we will not be causing harm to ourselves or others.

9. Instructing others in the Teachings – if you have gained knowledge you should pass it on. However, this is only when you have been asked. Buddhism does not encourage followers to go around preaching or trying to convert others.

10. Acting in Accord with the Teachings – this means we have to implement the teachings, and not just understand them intellectually. We should act in accord with the five precepts, four truths and the eightfold path and so forth.

If you wish to collect good imprints in your mind, this is the way to act. These imprints become more powerful when our actions are committed without the three poisons, which are attachment, aversion and unawareness.

The problem with only doing acts so as to get a better rebirth is that these acts are selfish, and so actually cannot really be called acts of merit. When we act in a selfish way we are not leaving positive imprints in our mind. In fact, it is the opposite.

If you see your mind as the pot and merit as positive imprints, I believe, you understand what Gautama Buddha taught about merit.

43

Rebirth Doesn't Matter

I was born into a Christian family and so my early experience of religion is being told I must be 'God fearing' and 'God moves in mysterious ways' – neither of these things moved me in any way. I attended church for christenings and weddings and found them to be bleak, unwelcoming and without any sense of warmth. I know others feel differently, but this was my personal experience. When I was eight I was taken out of Sunday school for asking too many questions. This left me feeling that something was missing in my life. So when I was older I embarked on a quest to find something to fill the void I felt inside.

This is when I came across Buddhism. It seemed to offer me all the things I was searching for. The two main points that stuck out for me were that I didn't have to believe in a god, and I had to take responsibility for my own actions and their consequences. It seemed like music to my ears. That was until I came across rebirth. Bam! I had hit a brick wall.

As much as I tried I couldn't get over or around this brick wall. It held me back for many years. Until one day a teacher told me to put it on the back burner and carry on with my studies and meditation practice. He advised me to revisit the concept of rebirth from time to time and see how I felt about it. This was excellent advice and I now give it to my students if they have difficulty with any part of Gautama Buddha's teachings.

Today, after 35 years of study and practice I still cannot buy into the concept of rebirth. However, it does not bother me anymore. I now understand that it does not matter if I believe it or not. What matters is that I am a good, kind and caring person in this life.

I honestly do not know if I have been born before or will be born again. What I do know is that I am alive now and so this life is what is important. Gautama Buddha stated this in the Apannaka Sutra:

> 'Even if one believes there is no other world, no future reward for helpful actions or punishment for harmful ones, still in this very life one can live happily, by keeping oneself free from anger, ill will and anxiety'.

I wish someone had shown me this quote 30 years ago. It would have saved me a whole lot of trouble. To me this quote is a win–win situation. By following Gautama Buddha's teachings we reduce our suffering now in this very life, and if there is a next life, we would have set ourselves up for a good rebirth. So whether you believe in rebirth or not, you will end up winning. That has to be a more realistic way of looking at rebirth.

It has taken me such a long time to get to this point, but finally, I understand that believing or not believing in rebirth really doesn't matter. Now I can concentrate on what really does matter, and that is reducing my suffering and the suffering of people around me.

Foot Note: When I first released this blog post I was heavily criticised. I was told I am not a monk, not a Buddhist and someone even suggested I was a devil. These are my own personal views and they may or may not be wrong, but they are how I feel. I never write anything in the hope of hurting someone else.

44

Keeping your mind positive

It is not possible to avoid negative thoughts entirely, because our brains are wired that way. However, it is possible to reduce their impact by being mindful. If we are aware we will be able to catch the negative thoughts and let them go. Below I have written a few techniques that I have personally found useful over the years.

Stop thinking in black and white

Life is not black and white; there is a very large grey area as well. When we are being negative we tend to think things are 'all or nothing' and 'this or that,' but that just isn't the case. We either think things are going to be perfect or a disaster, we never see the shades of grey between these two extremes.

When we are in a relationship, if we are being overly positive, we think it is going to be perfect. When we are being negative we think it is going to end in total heartache. However, there is a more realistic grey area between these two. If we are thinking realistically, we would see that sometimes the relationship will be fantastic, sometimes just good and other times not so good, just like every other relationship.

When you think in black and white terms you are setting yourself up for failure. Be realistic and think about the grey middle ground.

Befriend yourself

When other people make mistakes we tell them it doesn't matter and it is no problem. Yet, when we make the same mistake we are very harsh and unforgiving. We tell ourselves that we are stupid and we are always making mistakes. This is not only negative, but also destructive. You need to become your best friend and have compassion for yourself. You have to understand that you are human and so are liable to make mistakes from time to time. When you make a mistake just acknowledge it, learn from it and move on.

I would also add that if you know you are feeling negative, be kind to yourself and do not read or watch any news, as this could further irritate your mood.

Understand thoughts are just thoughts

We have to understand that a negative thought is just a negative thought. It only has power if we focus on it. If we blindly follow every negative thought we will never be able to be positive. If you think, 'I am a stupid person,' and you believe it, you are going to feel negative. However, if you just see a thought as a thought, you can say to yourself, 'I am thinking I am a stupid person at the moment.' There is a big difference between these two thoughts. If we see thoughts as a part of us we are going to follow every stupid thought we have – and let's face it, we have many.

Here is an example of believing thoughts to be real. We think we will not pass our exam and we get fixated on this thought. We tell ourselves that we are not good enough and we cannot remember what we have been taught. The more we follow these thoughts the more they become true. In the end, we totally believe we will fail the exam because we are stupid, and of course this type of negative thinking is just setting ourselves up for failure.

We have to understand that not everything we think is true, but we can only do this when we become mindful of our thoughts.

Use an affirmation

Next time you have a negative thought tell yourself, 'I am not a negative person. I am a positive person.' The mind will then start focusing on this thought and not the negative thought you were having. If you recite this affirmation every time you have a negative thought, slowly you will start to believe you are positive. You will be planting positive seeds into your mind and this will mean fewer and fewer negative thoughts will arise. The mind is a creature of habit, so encourage positive thoughts and avoid negative ones.

Don't accept other people's negativity

Let me start by telling you a story. This angry man approached Gautama Buddha and started shouting at him. Gautama Buddha just stood there and never got angry. The man was shocked. Gautama Buddha then asked the man this question, 'If you bought a present for someone but they didn't accept it, who does the present belong to?' the man replied, 'it belongs to me of course.' Gautama Buddha then said, 'It is the same with anger. If I do not accept it, the anger stays with you.'

It is actually the same with any negativity. We should not accept everything people try to dump on us. If someone is trying to tell you that you are not good at your job, but you know you are, then don't accept it. Tell yourself that this is just their opinion and it is not your experience. If we do not accept what is being offered, we will not take on other people's negativity.

Stop making up stories

Do any of these sound familiar?

- He hasn't called; it means he doesn't love me.

- She is late. She must be seeing someone else.

- If I was a good parent, I wouldn't get angry at the kids.

- I can't do this, so I must be stupid.

- My medical tests are not ready. It means I really am very sick.

We make up stories all the time and then start to believe them. It is true that life is not always a bowl of cherries, but it doesn't mean every situation is going to be bad. We have to deal with our experiences as they arise, and not invent a negative scenario, that may or may not happen.

Let's look at an example. You are driving to a business meeting and you take a wrong turn. The negative mind tells itself that you are always doing this, even though you aren't, and that you will now lose your job, which of course you won't. However, once we start thinking like this we get agitated and stressed. This leads to more negativity and so the downward spiral begins.

Keep your story telling for bedtime, and just respond to an experience as and when it arises.

List the positive

If you are a negative person it is useful to write a list of positive things in your life. This will help disarm your negative thinking. You can then refer to this list when you are feeling negative. You may think that no one loves you, but when you look at your list you see that your parents, family and friends all care for you. You may think that you are useless, but the list tells a different story – you went to a good university and you have a good job.

By referring to this positive list regularly you will be creating a natural defence against negativity. You will see that for every negative thought you may have, you will be able to counter them with four or five positive things in your life.

We have to be diligent if we wish to stop being carried away by negativity. We are responsible for what we think and so we are the ones that have to eliminate negative thoughts. With practice we will be able to see when we are thinking negative, and we can then implement the appropriate action. However, this all takes effort on our part, but reducing negativity and promoting positivity is totally doable.

45

Becoming your own Best Friend

I recently released a guided meditation practice entitled 'Befriending Yourself.' It got a huge reaction. Most of it positive, but some were asking questions like 'Why was it needed?' 'Isn't it a bit self-indulgent?' and 'Is it the same as self-esteem practices?' I will attempt to answer these questions in this blog post.

So firstly, what is befriending yourself? It is a practice whereby we have compassion for ourselves. We understand that we are going to make mistakes and when we do, instead of berating ourselves, we are kind and caring. We don't look to blame ourselves or others. We just understand that this is life and we learn from our mistakes and move on. We view our situation in a mindful way. It allows us to accept whatever we are going through non-judgementally. We are not suppressing or exaggerating the situation, we are just viewing it through compassionate and caring eyes.

I believe 'Befriending Yourself' is an extremely important practice, and this is why. Over the years I have found that we are very hard on ourselves. When we make a mistake, upset a loved one, put on a few pounds or keep getting carried away by strong emotions, we tend to be harder on ourselves than we would ever be on anyone else. If someone makes a mistake we tell them that it is fine and don't worry about it. However, if we make the same mistake we tell ourselves we are worthless, stupid or some other derogatory word. We may, mistakenly, believe talking to ourselves in such a way doesn't matter, but it does!

When we talk to ourselves in this way we become negative, and then it doesn't matter how good a person we are, how hard we try or how much effort we put in, it is never enough. Failure, no matter how large or small, is not acceptable to us, but failure is a part of life. It is a part of our human existence, because the world is an imperfect place. By being hard on ourselves, we are setting ourselves up to fail. We get trapped in a vicious circle of never ending self-abuse.

So we need to stop this destructive way of acting and start having compassion for ourselves. It seems that having compassion for others comes easy, but is very hard for ourselves. Compassion is the deep awareness of another's suffering, and an understanding that this person is human and so is imperfect. We have to have this same deep awareness of our own suffering and see our imperfections as a human condition, and not a personal thing. This is not being self-indulgent or having an over inflated sense of self-worth. It is being kind, caring and loving towards ourselves.

This is where Befriending Yourself is different from self-esteem practices. Self-esteem is based on how much we like or value ourselves, and what we are doing is actually evaluating ourselves against others. The world is so competitive these days and we think we have to be special, or at least above average. But that is a fool's game. How can we all be above average?

Because self-esteem is about puffing ourselves up, what we are subconsciously doing is putting others down. This can lead to aggression, prejudice, and dare I say it, narcissism.

Befriending ourselves isn't about being better than someone else, putting others down or judging ourselves against others. It is about understanding and accepting the imperfections of human life – our imperfections. It is about relating to ourselves in a non-judgemental way. If we decide to make changes it is because we care about ourselves, and understand that we are going through a difficult time at the moment. It certainly is not because we feel less than others or need to compete with someone. I personally see it as an emotional safety net or comfort blanket.

Life is not always going to be rosy. We are sometimes going to have off days, and it is during these times that we have to care for ourselves. The more we are able to open up to our human condition, the more we are able to have compassion for ourselves, and then for others. If we do not have compassion for ourselves, how can we have real compassion for others? We cannot give what we don't have. So become your own best friend and stop fighting this imperfect world.

You can find the 'Befriending Yourself' guided meditation practice here:

http://buddhismguide.org/guided-meditations/

Go on; try a bit of self-compassion today.

46

Reflect on your Values

As I was born into a Christian family I was taught the ten commandments from a very early age. I never liked being told 'Thou shalt not do this' and 'Thou shalt not do that,' it all seemed so final and restrictive. These commandments are fine if the world was black and white, but it isn't. It is impossible to divide our experiences into right and wrong, good and bad, correct and incorrect. There is a very large grey area in-between these extremes, and it is in this grey area we have to live our lives.

I much prefer Gautama Buddha's approach. When his son Rahula was eight years old he asked him what a mirror is for and Rahula answered that it is for reflecting. Gautama Buddha then went on to state that whenever engaging in an action of body, speech or mind , you should reflect, will this action bring harm to myself or others? If, after reflecting, you find that it will bring harm, then this action is not fit for you to do. However, if you find, after reflecting, that it is going to benefit you or others, then this action is fit for you to do. So he encouraged Rahula to train himself to constantly reflect on his physical, verbal and mental activities.

Why I like this is because it not only covers the black and white areas, the absolute notions of right and wrong, but also the large grey areas. Instead of trying to control his son with strict rules, he was asking him to reflect on harm and benefit.

However, if you are a person that likes rules then these two are all you need:

- Do not harm yourself or others
- Bring benefit to yourself and others

So use these two rules to help you reflect on your actions and see if they will bring harm or will bring benefit, that's it, you decide, not some ancient, outdated religion.

This approach allows you to cultivate responsibility, compassion, empathy and self-awareness. It does not restrict you to someone else's idea of right and wrong, it is giving you room to grow and form your own set of values.

This approach also helps guide you along the eightfold path. The path is a list of eight appropriate ways to conduct your life. So by reflecting on your actions, you are able to judge for yourself whether an action is appropriate or inappropriate. Again, if it is appropriate, go ahead and do it, because it will help you along the eightfold path. If, however, you deem the action to be inappropriate, do not do it, as it is not going to bring benefit to yourself or others, and it certainly is not going to take you down the right path.

When you reflect on your thoughts, feelings, emotions and actions, you are actually reflecting on your core values.

47

The Green-Eyed Monster

In the Jataka Tales there is a story about jealousy, called The Curse of Mittavinda, which is about a monk who lived in a tiny monastery in a little village. His alms food was always provided by the rich man of the village. In fact, all of his needs were looked after by the rich man, so the monk was calm and peaceful in his mind. There was no desire for greater comforts and pleasures. Instead, he was free to practice the correct conduct of a monk, always trying to eliminate his faults and do only wholesome deeds.

One day an elder monk arrived in the little village. When the rich man saw this unknown monk, he gave him food to eat, and he thought himself very fortunate to hear a short teaching from him. He then invited him to take shelter at the village monastery. When the visiting monk arrived at the monastery, he met the village monk. They greeted each other pleasantly. Then the village monk asked, "Have you had your lunch today?" The other replied, "Yes, I was given lunch by the supporter of this monastery. He also invited me to take shelter here." At this point, the village monk, who had been so contented, allowed the poison of jealousy to creep into his mind, he lost his former mental calm. His mind became disturbed due to his jealousy – the fear of losing his comfort and his daily food.

The next day, when it was time to go collect alms food from the supporter of the monastery, the village monk rang the temple gong, but he rang it by tapping it lightly with his finger nail. Then he went to the visiting monk's room and knocked on the door, but again he only tapped lightly with his finger nail. Having done his courteous duty in such a tricky way, he went to the rich man's home. The man bowed respectfully to the monk, took his alms bowl and asked, "Where is the new monk, our visitor?" The village monk replied, "I have not seen him. I rang the gong, I knocked at his door, but he did not appear."

The rich man then said,"Honourable monk, our holy visitor must be worn out from travelling. Please take my humble alms food to him." Saying nothing, he accepted the generous gift of food. On the way back to the monastery he saw a field that had just been burned by farmers to enrich the soil. It was covered with hot glowing coals. So he threw the rich man's generous gift on the coals. The alms food burned up without a trace. When he got back to the monastery, he found the visitor had gone, and so had his peace of mind! So, afraid of losing his easy daily food, he had thrown away his peace of mind. For the rest of his life the rich man continued to support him. But his mind was filled with torment and suffering, and because of his jealousy he felt doomed like a living hungry ghost.

That is the power of jealousy. It destroys our piece of mind, causes us to lose control and brings us untold suffering. In the English dictionary one definition of jealousy is 'an unhappy or angry feeling of wanting to have what someone else has, or an unhappy or angry feeling caused by the belief that someone you love (such as your husband/wife, friend and suchlike) likes or is liked by someone else.'

The definition in Buddhism goes further than this and explains that jealousy stems from attachment to an excessive preoccupation with 'me', 'I' or 'a permanent and solid self.' So, it not only explains what jealousy is, but also explains why we become jealous.

The problem is that we think 'I' am special and no one can do something, or love someone, as good as 'I' can. For example, people tell you that you cook great food and you start to believe you are the best cook around. Then one day, a friend cooks a meal and everyone says it is the best food they have ever tasted, you become jealous because your attachment to a sense of 'I' has been dented. Your feeling that you are special has taken a knock.

Another example is when we are in love and we think our partner only loves us, and we cannot believe they would ever love anyone else. When they leave us for another person, because of our attachment to 'I', we become wildly jealous.

Instead of rejoicing in other people's good fortune, because of jealousy, we become resentful, envious and are overwhelmed by destructive emotions. This is because jealousy is the inability to bear someone else's achievement and we actually wish we could achieve it instead.

The monk in the story above was attached to his good life and didn't want anyone to muscle in on his relationship with the rich man. This also goes back to him being attached to a sense of 'I.'

All these variations of jealousy stem from our attachment to the feeling of a permanent and solid 'I.' The way we can alleviate the problems and suffering caused by jealousy, is to treat the underlying misconception concerning 'I.' We have to start seeing everyone as equal. We need to understand that everyone has the same wish to be happy and not suffer. Also, it is important for us to realize that everyone has the same right to be happy and not to suffer. So, in this way, there is nothing special about 'me' in this regard.

When we learn to view everyone as equal it becomes easier to relate to someone who has either succeeded more than we have, or who has succeeded when we have not. We rejoice in his or her success, since we want everyone to be happy and not to suffer. Also, instead of gloating about having more success than someone else, we try to help them do well. This will help you to stop clinging to a sense of 'I' and, in turn, reduce your feelings of jealousy and give you peace of mind.

48

Who Gains from Forgiveness?

The act of forgiveness is an important one, but sometimes seems virtually impossible to do. This is because we think of forgiveness as an act we do for someone else. We feel like we are removing a burden from the other person, when in fact, we are actually removing a burden from ourselves. It is actually the giver of the forgiveness who needs the act to happen so they can move on with their lives.

The person who we feel has wronged us may have done it maliciously and does not care if we are suffering, or it may have been done innocently and the person is totally unaware of any harm caused. Either way it doesn't matter because we are aware and we are the ones carrying around feelings of resentment, pain, sadness, anger and even revenge. These destructive feelings are harming no one but ourselves, so it is clear forgiveness is going to be more beneficial to us and not the person who has caused us harm.

By releasing these negative feelings we are healing ourselves by stopping any tension related illnesses and make ourselves physically and spiritually well. When we free ourselves of this burden, we remove a heavy weight that is resting on our shoulders.

Now I understand that forgiveness is a complex subject and not a simple thing to do. It can take quite some time to feel released from the pain. You could be forgiving a small offence such as gossip or unkind words, or something more substantial like betrayal, rape or murder. It may have only happened once or is an ongoing thing. It could be current or happened many years ago. All of these factors make forgiveness extremely complex.

I believe there are two ways to help the forgiveness process. Firstly, there is reflection. This entails sitting quietly and looking within. It can be difficult to think clearly when we are hurting inside, so some quiet reflection helps to calm us down. Once you are calm and able to be more objective, ask yourself questions such as these:

Why am I finding it hard to forgive?

What emotions am I feeling regarding this situation?

Why should I forgive?

What are my past experiences with forgiveness?

What is stopping me from forgiving?

Who is going to benefit the most from my forgiveness?

Questions, such as these, will help you to gently start to let go and move on.

The second thing you can do to help with forgiveness is mindfulness. Being present in the moment cannot erase the past, but it will definitely assist you in responding more helpful to the emotions, thoughts and feelings you are experiencing. Here are a few strategies to try:

When you start to feel the suffering caused by the incident, take a few deep breathes and bring your focus back to the here and now. Place your attention on the breath entering and leaving your body. Let your shoulders relax and slowly feel yourself calm down. The pain you are feeling is in the past, so bring yourself into the present and let the painful feeling go.

Do a ten minute daily mindfulness practice, such as Fostering a Compassionate Mind or Cultivating Compassion in your Mind. These will help you move past any resentment you may have, and replace it with compassion, kindness and caring. Remember, compassion starts with yourself, so if you are having problems with this, try the Befriending Yourself practice.

If the incident is making you negative, try doing a Positive Breathing Awareness practice. This will help you let go of your negativity and replace it with a more positive and constructive attitude.

The thing to remember about forgiveness is that it is you that will be the main benefactor, and not the person who has wronged you. If you understand this, you will be able to start the process of forgiveness and healing.

All the above practices can be found here:

http://buddhismguide.org/guided-meditations/

About Karma Yeshe Rabgye

Karma Yeshe Rabgye is a Western Monk in the Kagyu tradition of Tibetan Buddhism. Originally from England, he now lives in Ashoka Buddhist Temple, Khuda Ali Sher, Northern India, where he teaches Buddhism and meditation classes to people of all ages.

Yeshe took ordination vows from H.E. Tai Situ Rinpoche in Sherabling Monastery, Northern India and has studied with H.H. The 14th Dalai Lama, H.H. The 17th Karmapa, H.E. Tai Situ Rinpoche, Khenpo Tsultrim Gyamtso Rinpoche, Dzongsar Jamyang Khyentse Rinpoche, Drupon Khenpo Lodro Namgial, Geshe Sonam Rinchen and Geshe Tashi Tsering. Having received teachings and studied works of all traditions of Buddhism, his books are inspired by successive short-term retreats in which Yeshe took the Buddha Shakyamuni's early teachings as his inspiration for practice.

Although Yeshe learnt from the great Tibetan Buddhist masters in exile, his Western background forced him to question some difficult elements of the teachings, in particular to distinguish those teachings that were essential aspects of the path from those that were mere cultural embellishments. Life's Meandering Path stems from this questioning and is aimed at a more secular and sceptical audience.

Yeshe spent several years in a monastery in the foothills of the Himalayas teaching young monks basic Buddhist philosophy and meditation. He now offers teachings freely to all in a manner that is unpretentious and clear. He does not demand students to blindly accept what he says, but instead invites them to examine their own minds and experiences to discover the validity of Gautama Buddha's teachings. Using everyday examples he has the ability to bring the teachings alive, particularly to a younger audience seeking to make Buddhism relevant in their lives. His approachable manner has attracted many students who appreciate his sense of humour and practical advice.

Yeshe quietly demonstrates Gautama Buddha's teaching on compassion through the charitable trust 'Sangye Menla' that he founded in 2008 in Chandigarh, Northern India. The trust provides medical assistance and care to people from the Himalayan region in India.

About the author's charity 'Sangye-Menla Trust'

The trust was set-up in 2008 by Karma Yeshe Rabgye and another Buddhist monk. It helps to facilitate the medical needs; including accommodation, doctor location, translation services, and often food for roughly 4000 people a year who travel with little or no money for much needed care. It helps people from the Himalayan regions that have to come to Chandigarh for medical treatment and do not know what hospital to attend, which doctor to see and where to stay. Often they do not speak Hindi or English and so cannot communicate their sickness to the doctors. The fully trained staff at Sangye Menla Trust interviews the patients on arrival and decide which is the best hospital and doctor for them. They will also attend the hospital with the patients to translate and ensure the patients understand their treatment. The trust also provides a very cheap hostel for the patients to stay in. They never turn anyone away and if the patients have no money they will offer free rooms and get sponsorship for treatment and medicines. Sangye Menla Trust was named by HH 17th Karmapa, kindly encouraging the Trust to put the aspirations of Sangye Menla (Medicine Buddha) into practice.

You can read more information or make a donation here: **www.medicinebuddhatrust.org**

43114119R00122

Made in the USA
Middletown, DE
30 April 2017